Ching's Everyday Easy Chinese

More Than 100 Quick & Healthy Chinese Recipes

CHING-HE HUANG

WM
WILLIAM MORROW
An Imprint of HarperCollinsPublishers

For all my family, friends, fans, and "gue-ren," thank you so much from my heart. A little bit more of me to you, with love.

First published in 2011 by HarperCollins UK as *Ching's Fast Food.*

CHING'S EVERYDAY EASY CHINESE. Copyright © 2011 by TZU London Ltd. All rights reserved. Printed in the United States of America. No part of this book may be used or reproduced in any manner whatsoever without written permission except in the case of brief quotations embodied in critical articles and reviews. For information address HarperCollins Publishers, 10 East 53rd Street, New York, NY 10022.

HarperCollins books may be purchased for educational, business, or sales promotional use. For information please write: Special Markets Department, HarperCollins Publishers, 10 East 53rd Street, New York, NY 10022.

FIRST U.S. EDITION

Photography © 2011 by Jamie Cho
Text, food, and styling © 2011 by Ching-He Huang
Designed by Sophie Martin and Joanna MacGregor

Library of Congress Cataloging-in-Publication Data

Huang, Ching-He.
  Ching's everyday easy Chinese : more than 100 quick & healthy Chinese recipes / Ching-He Huang.
      p. cm.
  1st US ed.
  Also published in 2011 by HarperCollins UK as Ching's fast food.
  Summary: "In her first US cookbook, Cooking Channel sensation Ching-He Huang demystifies classic Chinese dishes and shows readers how to make fresh, simple, delicious, and satisfying takeout food without leaving their homes."—Provided by publisher.
  Includes index.
  ISBN 978-0-06-207749-3
  1. Cooking, Chinese.   2. Cookbooks.   I. Title.
  TX724.5.C5.H78426 2011
  641.5951—dc23
                                                    2011014430

11 12 13 14 15   WBC/QG 10 9 8 7 6 5 4 3 2 1

introduction   7

Breakfast   15

Soups   27

Appetizers   39

Chicken & Duck   75

Beef, Pork & Lamb   97

Fish & Shellfish   119

Vegetarian   141

Specials   159

Rice   181

Noodles   193

Dessert   207

equipment   223
glossary   229
index   236
acknowledgments   240

Introduction

Enough is enough.

Chinese food doesn't get the recognition it rightly deserves in the Western world. French, Japanese, even Korean cuisine all receive high praise from food critics in the press, but Chinese food remains underappreciated. Chinese cuisine can be just as complex or as basic as any other cuisine. It has so much to offer and has given so much already. It has traveled all over the world with immigrant Chinese families and its influence can be seen in the food cultures of many different countries, from Asia—Japan, Thailand, Indonesia, and Vietnam—to the West.

Did you know that there are more takeout Chinese restaurants in America than every McDonald's, Burger King, and KFC put together? In the UK there are more than 15,000 Chinese takeout shops and restaurants, and Chinese takeout shops have officially overtaken Indian takeouts as the nation's favorite type of meal to order in every week. In America, Chinese restaurants first developed to provide food for the railway workers in the nineteenth century. Immigrant chefs had to use local ingredients to cater for their customers' tastes, so dishes were given a name and number and served with a very un-Chinese roll and butter. These were the circumstances in which Chinese takeout menus were first devised.

During this period and over the years, many inventive takeout dishes were created, including egg foo yung (omelette served with gravy), chow mein (stir-fried noodles), chop suey (leftovers in a brown sauce), crispy beef, and General Tso's chicken (battered chicken in a spicy sweet ketchup sauce)—dishes as well loved in Britain and America as shepherd's pie, pizza, or steak and potatoes.

If you are a fan of your local Chinese takeout shop and you then travel to China, my guess is that you will experience more than a culture shock, for the food will seem very unfamiliar. Some English businessmen have admitted to me that they fill their suitcases with chips and other goodies when they travel to China because they cannot stomach the food there! If you go with an open mind, however, you'll discover a whole new culinary world. Should you be lucky enough to dine with Chinese friends at their favorite Chinese haunt, you'll find the menu will be dismissed, there will be a few exchanges of Cantonese or Mandarin, some quick scribbles by the waiter, and you'll be treated to such delicacies as clay pot chicken, braised chicken's feet, "fish-fragrant" eggplant, steamed sea cucumbers, and baked salted chicken.

But there are signs that the disparity between takeout food and "real" Chinese cuisine is lessening. China has opened up over the last decade and there are now many more opportunities for travel to and from the country. The Internet has helped too. As a result, more people are beginning to appreciate that Chinese cooking is much more than what is served at their local takeout place.

Chinese takeout food has also recently moved on and become more exciting. There are more dim sum restaurants than ever, for instance, and while Cantonese cuisine is still the most widely served outside China, establishments offering dishes from other regions are sprouting up all over the place—no longer just Cantonese, but Sichuanese, Hunanese, Taiwanese, and Shanghainese. Chinese takeout food remains a huge phenomenon. Chinese takeouts can be found all over the world and each one has a unique story attached to it. Often you will hear how someone's grandfather started the takeout shop, or how the place has been in the same family for generations. By contrast, others have changed ownership many times, serving as a golden goose for perhaps a decade before being passed on.

When my family first arrived in England and we stood waiting for a train, I remember an elderly couple asking my father whether we owned a Chinese restaurant. That was two decades ago when it was the norm for newly arrived Chinese families to open a takeout shop. The majority of my father's friends in the Chinese community in London owned takeout shops.

In hindsight, my father thought he probably would have been more successful had he followed suit rather than going into the import–export business. At the time, however, he felt this was the right thing to do, as my grandparents were proud that their eldest son had graduated with a business degree and were prejudiced against him working in catering, which was considered laborious and low skilled (still the view in China today).

My first takeout experience was in England—at a small place on the Fortune Green Road in North London. Prior to that I had never had food from one. My mother is a great cook, and when we lived in South Africa (before traveling to England), she made all the meals. Her recipes were mainly Chinese but with a South African twist, such as a stir-fried or traditional stewed dish served with miele pap (rather like polenta) instead of boiled rice.

In fact, there were no Chinese takeouts that I can recall during my time in South Africa. There was only one Chinese supermarket in Jo'burg at the time, which my mum would religiously frequent every week to stock up on provisions for her Chinese larder.

In England, by contrast, there were a lot more takeout shops and one busy weekday, shortly after we had arrived in the country, we ordered from our local. The experience wasn't too bad, but Mum found it overly expensive and the fried rice not up to standard, so she turned her nose up at it and we never ordered from there again. The takeout shop remains in business, however: last time I passed, it was still there. Mum preferred the Cantonese restaurant, the Water Margin, on Golders Green Road, and we went there when she wasn't in the mood for cooking. The restaurant became the place where I could meet my friends (or a date) for a quick Saturday lunch while satisfying my craving for Cantonese roast duck on rice.

Chinese takeout shops are the "fast food" of Chinese cuisine. A takeout shop is where you would go to get your fried spring rolls, fried wontons, special fried rice, or beef with greens. It is usually a lot more salty and oily than home-cooked Chinese food, in which dishes are a lot simpler, less rich, and better balanced. It is no wonder that Chinese takeout shops have created a bad name for themselves, with many using high levels of monosodium glutamate to enhance the flavor. Although MSG is a natural substance, found in many foodstuffs, used as an additive it can have adverse effects. I personally have an intolerance to it, as it gives me heart palpitations and a dry throat.

To me, if you use the freshest ingredients, you don't need MSG because the dish will be full of flavor, especially if those ingredients are in season and at their very best. Many manufacturers of Chinese or Asian condiments often add MSG, and I have found that a small amount within a sauce is fine, but commercial sauces can contain quite a bit. Try to find ones that don't have MSG and contain ingredients that are as natural as possible. Best of all, create your own sauces—in this book I'll show you how to use pantry ingredients to make your own. It is true of all cuisines that the foods you cook yourself at home will be healthier and lighter than any takeout food. In fact, a recent report showed that a meal cooked at home contains on average 1,000 fewer calories than its takeout equivalent and considerably less salt. Even though my grandmother was partial to a little "gourmet powder" (MSG) from time to time, she always practiced what she preached—to be certain of what you're eating, it is better to cook the food yourself.

That's not to say that I'm not partial to Chinese takeout myself; indeed, there is a good one near where I live in North West London. I happen to know the owner and have been to the factory where the special 11-spice powder they use for their crispy aromatic duck is lovingly ground, and it's so good! When I don't have anything in my fridge or want to give myself time off from the kitchen, I just give them a ring and order number 15. But unless you know the establishment well, it's like takeout roulette, and we've all had a bad takeout experience at some time or another. If you have a reliable local takeout shop, support the owners and treat them like family!

I actually love Chinese food in all its forms—Americanized, anglicized, even bastardized. I recently had the pleasure of trying Chinese chicken salad American style and I could see the attraction in the sweet orange sauce coupled with crisp fried wonton skins, crunchy lettuce, and chicken strips. Yes, God forbid, I have even had a craving for it since! (I blame it entirely on the sugary sauce.) There is beauty in Chinese takeout food that is cooked well—even a pretty standard dish like sweet-and-sour pork balls. I know some expats living in Hong Kong who demand to have some of the anglicized takeout stuff and would import it if they could. It is simply a matter of taste. And what most fascinates me is how thousands of people all over the world are united in their love of Chinese takeout food, while the forefathers of this invention were completely unaware that they were the pioneers of Chinese fast food and the very best in their field. It is an amazing achievement when you think about it: these days R&D (research and development) chefs get paid six-figure sums to come up with what they did.

In my quest to share my love and appreciation of Chinese food, I myself have been blamed for "dumbing down" Chinese cuisine for the Western palate in my attempt to whet people's appetite for it. But I much prefer to see it as "creative fusion." If I remained true to the Chinese classics, I would be a copycat cook and not a progressive one. A cook's job in my opinion is to be creative and push the boundaries of their cuisine and never stop experimenting.

Yes, classics are good, but classics at one point in history came from somewhere too. They were once new—someone invented them, and if they had never experimented, we wouldn't be enjoying those dishes today.

And are classic dishes the only authentic ones? I prefer the term "heritage." Dishes can have heritage and influence, but they are not necessarily "authentic" because the

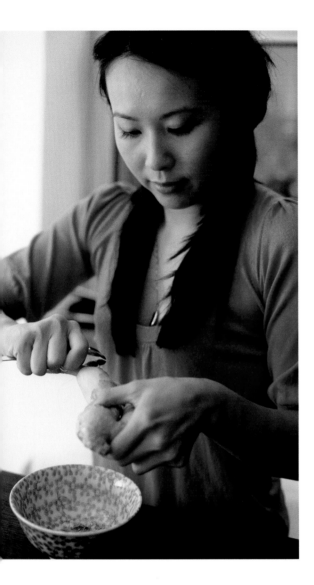

question would be, authentic to whom? Authenticity is a matter of perspective. Chinese takeouts have become such a staple of so many countries that you could argue that they are just as authentic within immigrant Chinese cooking as the older, classic dishes.

I am always being asked for takeout menu recipes, so here is my book on the subject. Don't accuse me of not knowing my *xiao long bao* from my *char siu bao*—because I do and I can make both. I want to share my love of Chinese takeouts and show how, cooked well, they can hold their own with the other great cuisines of the world. People also ask me whether I cook other types of food at home, and I certainly do. In fact, I have a soft spot for Lebanese cuisine, and I love Italian and Indian. But my vocation and career is making Chinese food—and please excuse the generic word "Chinese," for there are over 34 regions in China with over 54 different dialects, and each region has a unique way of preparing food. So until I master all the Chinese dishes there are to be mastered and explored, I won't be able to venture properly into other cuisines. Chinese cooking alone could keep me going for more than a lifetime.

If you are Chinese and, like my father, snobbish about Chinese takeout, my hope is that, after reading these recipes, you will be cooking and feeding them to your kids instead of the dog and you will feel encouraged to embrace them as part of your culture and be proud of them.

Chinese takeout cuisine is perfectly acceptable at home too, and I want to prove that, when cooked correctly, it can be the healthiest, most economical, and delicious food you have ever eaten. With many low-fat dishes and using plenty of fresh vegetables and lean meat and fish, it's also good for those who are worried about keeping slim. If you are vegetarian, Chinese food has a huge array of bean curd and "mock meat" recipes made from wheat gluten. Equally, if you are allergic to wheat or gluten or to monosodium glutamate, you can buy soy sauces that are wheat-free and condiments that don't contain MSG. If you have a nut allergy, use vegetable or sunflower oil instead of peanut oil, and if you are watching your salt intake, you can substitute a low-sodium, light soy sauce. I would also advise using organic or free-range eggs and meat wherever possible.

With this book, I want to give you my twenty-first-century version of Chinese takeout, inspired by this favorite fast food. I want to demonstrate how I think Chinese takeout dishes should be cooked at home. I will look at all the offerings, whether healthy or unhealthy, give my view on them, share tips with you, and show you lots of easy recipes that can be cooked far more quickly than it would take you to order your favorite takeout dish. I will share with you my knowledge of flavor pairings to get the best out of your Chinese pantry (see the box above for my top ten ingredients) and introduce some new ways of eating and cooking Chinese food. In addition, I want to show you how Chinese takeout dishes, when cooked with the freshest ingredients you can lay your hands on (coupled with the right culinary techniques), make for a far superior "fast food" than any other cuisine in the world. If I owned a takeout shop, the dishes in this book are the ones you'd find on my menu.

Enough said. Less talk and more cooking!

MY TOP TEN ESSENTIAL CHINESE PANTRY INGREDIENTS:

1. Light soy sauce
2. Dark soy sauce
3. Shaohsing rice wine
4. Toasted sesame oil
5. Five-spice powder
6. Sichuan peppercorns
7. Chinkiang black rice vinegar
8. Clear rice vinegar
9. Chili bean sauce
10. Chili sauce

= vegetarian

= contains chili

Ching x

Breakfast

When I first arrived in South Africa, I was five and a half. After a tearful good-bye to the rest of the family, my mother, brother, and I packed our bags to join my father, who had already left to set up a bicycle business in South Africa. In Taiwan he had been working as a manager in a building company and hated his job. So when by chance he met Robert ("Uncle Robert" to us) and the South African convinced my father to set up in business with him, he jumped at the idea. We liked Uncle Robert: we had met him only once, but he had taken us to a pizza restaurant and given me a cuddly raccoon toy from South Africa. Despite no previous business experience and not knowing a word of English, my father moved us all over there on a whim. It was to be one of the scariest but most fulfilling adventures of my childhood.

At Uncle Robert's insistence, we stayed on his farm just outside Jo'burg. He and his wife, Susan, accommodated us in a converted barn on their plot of land, which extended for acres and acres. They even had a mini reservoir with their own supply of water and they kept horses and several Rhodesian Ridgebacks. Aunty Susan was a welcoming lady. The day we arrived, while my mother was unpacking and tidying up the barn, she took us food shopping. My brother and I were taken to the most enormous building we had ever seen. It was a hypermarket. Back in Taiwan, I hadn't even been to a supermarket before. Even in Taipei, the only modern outlets we had were 7-Eleven convenience stores. The only place like it in our experience was the local open market my grandmother used to take us to in the village, so this vast building was a shock.

My brother and I went up and down the aisles, admiring the rows and rows of packaged ingredients. There were even fish tanks with fresh lobsters and crabs. Aunty Susan guided us to a large chilled section; I remember feeling really cold. She pointed to the shelves and gestured to us to pick something, so I picked a small light brown carton and my brother picked a dark brown one. We hadn't a clue what we had chosen. The rest of that shopping trip is now hazy, although I remember plenty of boxes and paper bags being carted to Aunty Susan's large fancy kitchen.

She handed us each a teaspoon and we left her to her unpacking. I opened the foil lid of my carton and took a small mouthful, and my brother did the same. The taste was creamy and sour but also sweet; I had no idea that I had picked a caramel-flavored yogurt and my brother a chocolate one. We were used to our Yakult, but this was an entirely new experience. We weren't sure we liked it, but we went back to the barn and showed the yogurts to Mum. She took a small mouthful and then spat it out: "*Pai kee yah!*" ("It's gone off!" in Taiwanese). She stormed over to Aunty Susan's and started "communicating" with her. They couldn't understand what each other was saying; in the end my mum threw the pots in the garbage! Aunty Susan looked bewildered and shrugged her shoulders. I thought Mum was rude, but I didn't dare say anything. The next day Aunty Susan dropped by as Mum was making us fried eggs for breakfast. She brought over these dark green vegetables, which my mum called *hulu-* or gourd-shaped. Aunty Susan sliced one in half to reveal a large round pit in the middle; she then scooped the green flesh out of one of the halves and smeared it onto a slice of brown bread she had brought over with her. She gestured to my mother to take a bite. My mum had a taste and shook her head, saying, "*Bu hao chi*" ("Not good eat"). "Avocaaaa-do," said Aunty Susan, then smiled, patted us on our heads, and walked out the door.

Despite not liking the taste, my mother hated wasting food, so she placed the eggs she had been frying on the avocado bread, drizzled over some soy sauce, and told us to eat it. She didn't have any herself. Over time, however, avocados became one of my mum's favorite foods. She now lives permanently in Taiwan, where avocados are hard to get and expensive. When we Skype, she will often ask, "You still eating avocados?" That recipe, washed down with a glass of soy milk, is now one of my favorite dishes for breakfast.

You will notice that my recipes, like yin and yang, tend to be very black and white, very Western or very Chinese, but when recipes work together, East and West can be balanced, like the takeout menu, to give amazing, what I like to call "fu-sian"-style food. You may not associate breakfast with Chinese takeout, but there are many eateries all over Asia that serve warming breakfasts that can be bought on the way to school or work. In addition to Western-style sandwiches, these small eateries (and sometimes street stalls) serve *you-tiao*, or fried bread sticks, with hot or cold soy milk (sweetened or unsweetened), *mantou* (steamed buns) with savory or sweet fillings, and of course steaming bowls of congee in a variety of flavors. If I had a takeout shop or diner, I would definitely include a breakfast menu, and I would serve a variety of Western- and Chinese-style treats—just like the snack stalls in the East.

Toast with avocado, fried eggs, and soy sauce

Aunty Susan, whom we stayed with when we first arrived in South Africa, once gave my mother two ripe avocados, smearing one of them on some bread. Mum thought it was odd to serve a vegetable in this way, but soon she started to make us fried-egg sandwiches for breakfast with a generous slathering of avocado. Now I don't hesitate to make this for breakfast, spreading slices of toast with a chunky rich layer of ripe avocado, topped with poached or fried eggs (preferably sunny-side up) and a drizzle of light soy sauce. If I had my own takeout shop or diner, this would certainly feature on the menu!

PREP TIME: 5 minutes • **COOK IN:** 3 minutes • **SERVES:** 1

1 tbsp of peanut oil

2 large eggs

2 slices of seeded rye bread

½ ripe avocado (save the rest for a salad later), pit removed and flesh scooped out

Drizzle of light soy sauce

Salt and ground black pepper

1. Heat a wok over medium heat until it starts to smoke and then add the peanut oil. Crack the eggs into the wok and cook for 2 minutes or to your liking. (I like mine crisp underneath and still a bit runny on top.) Meanwhile, place the bread in the toaster and toast for 1 minute.

2. To serve, place the toast on a plate and spread with the avocado flesh. Place the eggs on top and drizzle over the soy sauce, then season with salt and ground black pepper and eat immediately. This is delicious served with a glass of cold soy milk, a cup of rooibos tea with a slice of lemon, or some freshly pressed apple or orange juice.

Basil omelette with spicy sweet chili sauce

In Taiwan, there are many night market stalls that sell the famous oyster omelette. A little cornstarch paste is stirred into beaten eggs, then small oysters are added and sometimes herbs. When the eggs have almost set, a spicy sweet chili sauce is drizzled over the top, making a comforting, addictive snack. I adore this dish, but it is hard to get fresh small oysters, so I sometimes make a vegetarian version for breakfast, using sweet basil and free-range eggs, and adding my own spicy sweet chili sauce, made using condiments from my Chinese pantry.

PREP TIME: 3 minutes • **COOK IN:** 5 minutes • **SERVES:** 1

3 eggs

Large handful of Thai or Italian sweet basil leaves

Pinch of salt

Pinch of ground white pepper

1 tbsp of peanut oil

Handful of mixed salad leaves, to garnish

FOR THE SAUCE

1 tbsp of light soy sauce

1 tsp of vegetarian oyster sauce

1 tbsp of mirin

1 tsp of tomato ketchup

1 tsp of Guilin chili sauce, or other good chili sauce

1. Make the spicy sweet chili sauce by whisking all the ingredients together in a bowl, then set aside.

2. Crack the eggs into a bowl, beat lightly, and add the basil leaves, then season with the salt and ground white pepper.

3. Heat a wok over high heat until it starts to smoke and then add the peanut oil. Pour in the egg and herb mixture, swirling the egg around the pan. Let the egg settle and then, using a wooden spatula, loosen the base of the omelette so that it doesn't stick to the wok. Keep swirling any runny egg around the side of the wok so that it cooks. Flip the omelette over if you can without breaking it, then fold and transfer to a serving plate, drizzle over some of the spicy sweet chili sauce, and serve with a garnish of mixed salad leaves.

Smoked salmon and egg fried rice

This is my classic breakfast recipe—it's so good I had to share it with you. Make sure you add the smoked salmon after the rice, as the rice acts as a cushion, helping the salmon not to catch on the side of the wok and flake into tiny pieces.

PREP TIME: 5 minutes • **COOK IN:** 7 minutes • **SERVES:** 1

1½ tbsps of peanut oil

2 eggs, beaten

3 oz frozen peas

11 oz cold leftover cooked jasmine rice (see the first tip on page 186) or freshly cooked long-grain rice (see the tip below)

5 oz smoked salmon, sliced into strips

1–2 tbsps of light soy sauce

1 tbsp of toasted sesame oil

Pinch of ground white pepper

1. Heat a wok over high heat until it starts to smoke and then add 1 tbsp of the peanut oil. Add the beaten eggs to the wok and stir for 2 minutes or until they are scrambled, then remove from the wok and set aside.

2. Return the wok to high heat and add the remaining peanut oil, allowing it to heat for 20 seconds. Add the frozen peas and stir-fry for just under a minute. Add the cooked rice and mix well until the rice has broken down.

3. Add the smoked salmon slices and toss together for 1 minute, then add the scrambled egg pieces back into the wok and stir in. Season with the soy sauce (to taste), the toasted sesame oil, and white pepper and serve immediately.

> **CHING'S TIP**
> If using freshly cooked rice, use 5 oz of uncooked long-grain rice, such as basmati, rinse it well, and then boil in 1¼ cups of water, cooking until all the water has been absorbed. This will take an extra 20 minutes.
>
> **ALSO TRY**
> If you are not a fan of fish, then use smoked bacon lardons instead—cook them until crisp before adding.

Country sausage, green pepper, and tomato fried rice with pineapple

A few years ago, I came up with bacon and egg fried rice, which my friends adored. This one is a follow-up recipe. It's the ultimate brunch dish—so easy to do on a lazy Sunday. Children will love it and the neighbors will hate you as they spy enviously over the fence while you dig in. This is my equivalent of a fry-up, but avoid using too much oil in this dish, as the sausages are quite fatty. It's best to pour the excess fat away, as described below. For a healthier version of this dish, you could mix in some spinach leaves if you liked and serve with a simple garden salad.

PREP TIME: 10 minutes • **COOK IN:** 7 minutes • **SERVES:** 4

2 cloves of garlic, finely chopped

1-inch piece of fresh ginger, peeled and thinly sliced into matchsticks

6 country sausages (12 oz in total), chopped into ½-inch rounds

1 green pepper, seeded and cut into ½-inch dice

1 very large ripe beefsteak tomato, cut into chunks

1 lb 2 oz cold leftover cooked jasmine rice (see the first tip on page 186) or freshly cooked long-grain rice (see the tip below)

1 tbsp of light soy sauce

1 tbsp of chili oil

Juice of 1 lemon

Large handful of ripe pineapple chunks

1. Heat a wok over high heat until it starts to smoke. Add the garlic and ginger and stir-fry for a few seconds, then add the sausages and cook over medium heat for 3–4 minutes, stirring constantly. Remove from the heat and pour away the excess oil.

2. Return the wok to the heat, add the pepper, and stir-fry for 1–2 minutes, then add the tomato and toss all the ingredients together. Add the cooked rice, breaking it up well, especially if it has been in the fridge overnight.

3. Season with the soy sauce, chili oil, and lemon juice, then mix in the pineapple chunks, remove from the heat, and serve immediately. Delicious with a glass of cold lemonade.

> **CHING'S TIP**
> If using freshly cooked rice, use 9 oz of uncooked long-grain rice, such as basmati, rinse it well, and then boil in 2¼ cups of water, cooking until all the water has been absorbed. This will take an extra 20 minutes.

Pork, ginger, and duck egg congee

This is one of my favorite breakfast dishes. The famous *cha chaan teng* tea restaurants in Hong Kong serve it, especially the ones located in the old open market at Canton Road in Kowloon. I love visiting the open markets there; I usually go shopping early for ingredients and then reward myself with a steaming bowl of this congee.

PREP TIME: 10 minutes • **COOK IN:** 65 minutes • **SERVES:** 4–6

2 century eggs, each sliced into quarters and halved lengthwise

1 tbsp of peanut oil

1-inch piece of fresh ginger, peeled and thinly sliced

7 oz pork tenderloin, thinly sliced

1 tbsp of Shaohsing rice wine, dry sherry, or vegetable stock

3 shiitake mushrooms, finely diced

2 tbsps of light soy sauce

Salt and ground white pepper

Dash of toasted sesame oil (optional)

2 scallions, thinly sliced, to garnish

FOR THE CONGEE

9 oz jasmine rice or 7 oz jasmine rice and 2 oz glutinous rice

Generous 1 cup vegetable stock

1. First make the congee. Pour the rice into a large heavy-bottomed saucepan, add the stock and 3 cups of water, and bring to a boil. Once boiling, reduce the heat to medium-low, place a tight-fitting lid on the pan, and allow to simmer, stirring occasionally to make sure the rice does not stick to the side and bottom of the pan.

2. After the rice has been cooking for 45 minutes, add the duck egg pieces and continue to cook for an additional 20 minutes.

3. Meanwhile, heat a wok over high heat until it starts to smoke. Add the peanut oil and ginger slices and stir-fry for a few seconds, then add the pork slices and stir for 1 minute, or until they start to turn brown. Add the rice wine (or sherry or vegetable stock) and cook for an additional minute, then add the mushrooms and season with the soy sauce.

4. Add the pork stir-fry to the cooked congee and stir in well. Season with salt and pepper, add a dash of sesame oil, if you like, and sprinkle over the sliced scallions. Serve immediately with chunks of *you-tiao* (fried bread sticks), if you have any, for a truly traditional Chinese breakfast.

Big bowl of oat congee and accompaniments—"The Works"

This is not for the faint-hearted—like eating "smelly porridge," as my other half describes it. But if you are a fan of durian, stinky tofu, and century eggs, then you will love the complex flavors of this dish. The fermented bean curd blends in with the sweetness of the seaweed paste and picks up the fiery pungency of the pickled bamboo shoots, while the pickled lettuce delivers a refreshingly vinegary sweetness that cuts through the richness of all the other ingredients.

This dish brings back memories and instantly I am transported to my grandmother's farm, where daily breakfast treats would be a rotation of these ingredients, along with a small bowl of hot steaming congee (or rice porridge). Rice porridge takes too long for me to make in the morning, so I now have oat porridge instead. When I prepare this, assembling all the ingredients, it is like a meditation process and nostalgia trip rolled into one. Nothing can get in the way and I feel depressed when I run out of any of the components. You may be surprised and perhaps even disgusted by this strange obsession of mine, but I invite you to try the dish with courage and an open mind.

PREP TIME: 5 minutes • **COOK IN:** 6 minutes • **SERVES:** 1

3½ oz rolled oats

1 tbsp of peanut oil

2 eggs

5–6 chives or 1 scallion, finely chopped (optional)

1 tbsp of light soy sauce

FOR THE ACCOMPANIMENTS

4–5 pickled soy lettuce stems

1 tsp of momoya (Japanese seaweed paste)

1 tbsp of salted roasted peanuts

1 tbsp of pickled bamboo shoots in chili oil

2 tbsps of dried pork floss

½ small cube of tofu ru (fermented bean curd)

1. Place the oats in a saucepan with a generous cup of water and bring to a boil, then reduce the heat and cook for 3–4 minutes, stirring frequently, or until the mixture has thickened.

2. Meanwhile, heat a small wok or skillet over medium heat until it starts to smoke and then add the peanut oil. Crack in the eggs, sprinkle over the chopped chives or scallion (if using), and fry the eggs to your liking.

3. Transfer to a plate and drizzle over the soy sauce. Pour the porridge into a bowl, arrange all your accompaniments on top (like the different colors on a painter's palette), and then mix and eat right away with the eggs.

Soups

I adore Chinese soups—the classic takeout offerings and the more exotic ones. The nourishing soups my grandmother used to make for me using Chinese herbs like cassia twigs, red dates, *Angelica sinensis*, rhizome of rehmannia, and others that I cannot pronounce were a staple in my family kitchen. Both my mother and grandmother insisted that we have these herbal broths, often cooked with a little meat, such as *lao-ji* (old organic chicken) or *pai-gu* (pork ribs). This was based on the belief that these traditional Chinese herbs replenish the "yang" *chi* (energy) thought to be good for a woman's "system," keeping her fertile and youthful. My grandmother especially loved stewing these herbal concoctions and the meat she typically included would be pig's trotters or chicken's feet, believing that their gelatinous texture would help keep skin plump and beautiful—and I believe her, because grandmothers always know best. I never argued with my grandmother when it came to food; she was the food royalty in my family, the queen bee, and her opinion was always the final word on the subject.

I grew up not turning my nose up at such dishes because this was the norm in my family. I only realized that these treasured family recipes were "different" when my school friend Lina came over for dinner one Saturday night. I had recently moved from South Africa to London and had just started secondary school. Lina, of Lebanese origin, was the bubbliest girl at school and one of the most popular, so I was excited that she was coming round. My mother went to a Chinese supermarket and brought back the

freshest ingredients. When asked what we were having for dinner, my mother pointed to a shiny red bucket with a bamboo steamer lid over it. We both took a peek and, to Lina's horror, were greeted by two fat river eels writhing about in the water and staring up at us. My mum was planning to cook herbal eel soup for us. I will never forget the look on Lina's face! Needless to say, she didn't stay for dinner and didn't come round again for a very long time, let alone for dinner. When she eventually invited me to her house, I was greatly relieved that the "eel experience" had not damaged our friendship.

Her family was so welcoming. It was a treat to watch her mother make hummus from scratch, her *tete* (grandmother) make the flatbread and tabouleh, and her father orchestrate the cooking of shish taouk and lamb shawarmas on their gigantic home-built barbecue. Everything smelled wonderful. We all sat around a large table and feasted together. Her father, a proud, eccentric man, made sure I had plenty to eat and my plate stayed full. I was enjoying everything until he winked at me to try a dish of what looked like very small sausages, so I did. The whole room exploded in laughter; her brother patted me on my back and declared, "How were the sheep's testicles, Ching?!" Wide-eyed, I turned to look at him and nearly spat the piece of "sausage" in his face. So Lina and I were even, and neither episode was ever mentioned again.

Lina and I continued to have many more culinary adventures together as our friendship developed. I once tried making her and some other school friends chicken and sweetcorn soup, which was far too watery because it was the first large-batch cooking I had ever attempted. When we reached sixth grade, sometimes we had no classes after lunch, so we would hitch the 240 bus from Mill Hill to Golders Green in search of satisfying our cravings for wonton soup or beef and black bean soup with ho fun noodles. Our destination was the Water Margin in Golders Green, where we would gossip about school or pour our hearts out over boys we fancied while sipping from a bowl of crabmeat and corn soup or hot and sour soup, dishes that comforted us and seemed to echo the sour-sweet times as teenagers living in London and trying to fit in. We fought to fit in at school, struggling with our cultural differences and desperate to find our identity, but food connected us.

My mother's herbal eel soup may have tested my friendship with Lina, but it will always remind me of who I am and where I come from. I believe the strongest relationships are built on such experiences. I once overheard my mother on the phone to her friend; they were talking about a lady within the Chinese community whose English husband was apparently filing for divorce because he had caught her eating fish-head soup! The lesson I learned was that if those close to you accept your food choices, no matter how weird, they are true friends. In case you want to test this out yourself, I have included Mum's Herbal Eel Soup (see page 37) for you to try.

One thing is for sure, when I'm feeling under the weather, when there are dramas going on, or I'm plagued by worry, I always make a comforting bowl of soup and I get my perspective back again. I have included some of my takeout favorites here and given some a makeover.

Tomato and egg flower soup

Classic egg flower or egg drop soup (*dan hua tang*)—"egg flower" describing the web-like pattern made by the egg when dropped into the hot liquid—is easy to make and very nutritious. You can add other ingredients to this soup, such as cubes of fresh tofu, baby shrimp, or dried seaweed (nori), or, for a more substantial dish, cooked egg noodles for a quick, light supper.

PREP TIME: 5 minutes • **COOK IN:** 10 minutes • **SERVES:** 2

1 tbsp of vegetable bouillon powder or stock powder

3 ripe tomatoes, sliced (see the tip below)

2 eggs, lightly beaten

1 tbsp of light soy sauce

Dash of toasted sesame oil

Pinch of sea salt

Pinch of ground white pepper

1 tbsp of cornstarch mixed with 2 tbsps of water

Large handful of baby spinach (optional)

2 scallions, thinly sliced, to garnish

1. Pour 2¼ cups of water into a large saucepan and bring to a boil. Add the bouillon or stock powder and stir to dissolve. Reduce the heat to a simmer, then add the tomatoes and cook over medium heat for 5 minutes, or until the tomatoes have softened.

2. Pour the beaten eggs into the broth, stirring gently. Add the soy sauce, toasted sesame oil, salt, pepper, and cornstarch paste and mix well until slightly thickened. Add the spinach (if using) and let it wilt, then garnish with the scallions and serve immediately.

> **CHING'S TIP**
> I don't bother skinning tomatoes—most of the nutrients are just beneath the skin after all—but if you want to skin them before slicing, first cut a small cross at the base of each tomato. Plunge them into a wok or saucepan of boiling water for less than 1 minute, then drain. The skin will peel off easily.

Traditional hot and sour soup

This is one of my all-time favorite soup recipes. It transforms pantry staples into an amazing dish. There may seem to be a long list of ingredients, but the end result is worth it because they all help to create layers of flavor and texture in this wonderfully warming winter dish.

PREP TIME: 20 minutes • **COOK IN:** 20 minutes • **SERVES:** 4

1 tbsp of vegetable bouillon powder or stock powder

1 tbsp of peeled and grated fresh ginger

2 red chilies, seeded and finely chopped

11 oz cooked chicken breast, shredded

1 tsp of Shaohsing rice wine or dry sherry

2 tbsps of dark soy sauce

One 8-oz can of sliced bamboo shoots, drained

⅓ oz dried Chinese wood ear mushrooms, soaked in hot water for 20 minutes, drained and thinly sliced

3½ oz fresh firm tofu, cut into ½ x 2-inch strips

2 oz Sichuan preserved vegetables, rinsed and sliced (optional)

2 tbsps of light soy sauce

3 tbsps of Chinkiang black rice vinegar or balsamic vinegar

1 tbsp of chili oil

Few pinches of white pepper

1 egg, lightly beaten

1 tbsp of cornstarch mixed with 2 tbsps of water

1 large scallion, sliced

Handful of chopped cilantro, to garnish (optional)

1. Pour 4¼ cups of water into a large saucepan and bring to a boil. Add the bouillon or stock powder and stir to dissolve. Bring back up to a boil and then add all the ingredients up to and including the wood ear mushrooms. Reduce the heat to medium, then add the tofu, Sichuan vegetables (if using), soy sauce, vinegar, chili oil, and white pepper and simmer for 10 minutes.

2. Stir in the egg, then add the cornstarch paste and stir to thicken the soup (adding more cornstarch paste if you like a thicker consistency). Add the scallion, garnish with the cilantro, if you like, and serve immediately.

> **CHING'S TIP**
> If you love your spicy heat, just increase the amount of chilies.
>
> **ALSO TRY**
> You can substitute shiitake mushrooms for the chicken for a vegetarian version of this dish.

Watercress soup with pork, mushroom, and ginger wontons

Probably one of the most popular takeout soups, this is also a personal favorite. I love these dumplings in a clear broth. The ones we used to have at the Water Margin were large and plump with a shrimp and pork filling. This is my version; I like making mine small using small wonton egg wrappers, which you can easily pick up from a Chinese supermarket. The beauty of this dish is that you can serve it for a casual dinner or an elegant supper—versatile, like a pair of trusted black patent Fendi boots.

PREP TIME: 20 minutes • **COOK IN:** 10 minutes • **SERVES:** 4

28 wonton wrappers
(3 inches square)
1 egg, beaten
3 cups vegetable stock

FOR THE FILLING
9 oz ground pork
1 large scallion, finely
chopped
3 shiitake mushrooms, finely
diced
1 tbsp of peeled and grated
fresh ginger
1 tbsp of Shaohsing rice wine
or dry sherry
1 tbsp of cornstarch
Pinch of sea salt
Pinch of ground white pepper

TO SERVE
1–2 tbsps of toasted sesame oil
Small handful of watercress
leaves
1 scallion, thinly sliced

1. Place all the ingredients for the filling in a large bowl and mix together well.

2. To prevent the wrappers from opening up once cooked, brush the inside of each one with some of the beaten egg. Take one wonton wrapper and place a small teaspoon of the filling in the center. Gather up the sides of the wrapper and mold around the filling into a ball shape, twisting the top to secure it. Repeat with the remaining wrappers.

3. To make the soup, pour the stock into a large saucepan and bring to a simmer. Add the wonton dumplings and cook for 5 minutes, or until they all rise to the surface—like floating clouds, as the Chinese might say.

4. Pour the soup and dumplings into serving bowls, allowing 7 dumplings per person. Add a dash of toasted sesame oil to each bowl, scatter over a few of the watercress leaves (letting them wilt in the bowl), finish with a sprinkling of sliced scallion, and serve immediately.

> **CHING'S TIP**
> If any filling is left over, make more dumplings and freeze. They can be cooked from frozen for an emergency supper.

Pork rib, turnip, and carrot broth with cilantro

This is one of my grandfather's favorite recipes. It is not standard takeout fare, but there are many takeout and eat-in restaurants in Taiwan that serve this kind of pork rib soup (*pai-gu tang*) to accompany salty main dishes. Eaten between mouthfuls of the main dish, it works as a palate cleanser. It is a light sweet broth, the daikon (white radish) adding a slight bittersweetness to complement the meatiness of the pork ribs. When I eat it, it always reminds me of my grandmother's home cooking. If I had my own takeout shop, this soup would be on the menu, no question.

PREP TIME: 10 minutes • **COOK IN:** 25 minutes • **SERVES:** 4

9 oz pork ribs, cut into 1-inch pieces

2 tbsps of vegetable bouillon powder or stock powder

12 oz daikon (white radish), sliced into ½-inch rounds, each cut into 6 wedges

2 carrots, cut into ½-inch rounds, each quartered into wedges

1 tbsp Shaohsing rice wine or dry sherry

Sea salt and ground white pepper

Handful of roughly chopped cilantro

1. Prepare the pork ribs by blanching them in boiling water for 2 minutes and draining well. Bring 4¼ cups of water to a boil in a large saucepan and add the bouillon or stock powder, stirring it to dissolve.

2. Add the pork ribs, daikon, carrots, and rice wine or dry sherry. Bring back up to a boil, then reduce the heat to medium-low and simmer for 20 minutes, or until the vegetables are tender. Season with salt and ground white pepper, add the chopped cilantro, and serve immediately.

Posh crab and crayfish tail corn soup

To me, a good takeout shop would serve this soup. It may be relatively expensive, but it is so worth it. I usually have a few cans of crabmeat and corn in my pantry and this makes a delicious quick, light supper. If you are entertaining, you can jazz up this recipe by topping it with some shredded cooked lobster tails and serving with some toasted rye bread and butter. You could also substitute fresh crabmeat for the canned crabmeat for a treat.

PREP TIME: 5 minutes • **COOK IN:** 15 minutes • **SERVES:** 4

Two 6-oz cans of crabmeat in brine, drained
One 15-oz can of corn kernels, drained
1 large ripe tomato, sliced
2 eggs, beaten
3 tbsps of light soy sauce
1 tbsp of toasted sesame oil
Sea salt and ground white pepper
2 tbsps of cornstarch mixed with ¼ cup of water
1 large scallion, thinly sliced
6½ oz cooked crayfish tails in brine, drained

1. Pour 4¼ cups of water into a large wok or saucepan and bring to a boil. Add the crabmeat, corn, and tomato and bring back up to a boil, then reduce the heat and simmer for 5 minutes.

2. Add the beaten eggs and stir gently to create a web-like pattern in the soup as the eggs start to cook. Season with the soy sauce, sesame oil, salt, and pepper, adding more to taste if necessary. Bring to a boil and then stir in the cornstarch paste to thicken the soup. Reduce the heat, sprinkle in the scallion, and leave to simmer over low heat until ready to serve.

3. Ladle the soup into serving bowls, top with a few crayfish tails (which will warm through in the heat of the soup), and serve immediately.

> **ALSO TRY**
> You could substitute cooked sliced chicken breast for the crabmeat or, for a vegetarian option, use diced marinated tofu or sliced shiitake mushrooms (or button mushrooms if you are on a budget). If you want a creamier consistency, use a can of creamed corn instead.

Mum's herbal eel soup

I wanted to include this more unusual recipe even though it doesn't really have a connection to Chinese takeout in the West. In Hong Kong, on the other hand, there are eateries that serve herbal soups such as this for takeout. Don't be put off by the sound of this soup—it's actually quite delicious, although admittedly an acquired taste. You will either love or hate it—for me, it's love. It's also very good for you. If you can, add a few dried goji berries to the soup 15 minutes before the cooking time is up; they lend a mellow sweetness to the broth. These, together with the other herbs, can be bought from a Chinese supermarket.

PREP TIME: 5 minutes • **COOK IN:** 65 minutes • **SERVES:** 4

1 lb 5 oz fresh river eel, head and tail discarded and any fins removed (or ask your fishmonger to do this for you)

2 tbsps of Shaohsing rice wine or dry sherry

½ tsp of salt

1 tbsp of vegetable bouillon powder or stock powder

¼ oz *Angelica sinensis* (Chinese angelica or dong quai)

¼ oz rhizome of rehmannia

⅓ oz *Ligusticum wallichii* (Sichuan lovage)

¼ oz matrimony vine

5 dried red dates

Two 2-inch sticks of cassia

One 2-inch stick of cinnamon

Small handful of dried goji berries (optional)

1. Slice the eel into 2-inch pieces, keeping the bones intact, then rinse well. Place the pieces in a large saucepan of boiling water to blanch for 2 minutes and then drain and set aside.

2. Place the blanched eels back in the pan. Pour in 6¼ cups of water and add all the remaining ingredients except the goji berries. Bring to a boil, then reduce the heat and simmer for 1 hour or until the eel is tender and delicious. If using the goji berries, add these for the final 15 minutes of cooking.

> **ALSO TRY**
> If you're not so keen on the idea of cooking eel, then simply substitute chicken or pork ribs.

Appetizers

No, Peking duck is better." This is what my father would insist whenever he saw crispy aromatic duck on the menu at a Chinese restaurant. On one occasion I felt I had to intervene; I could see the disappointed look on the Swiss husband of one of my father's guests. I told my father I had a craving for crispy duck and he called me a *wai guo ren* (foreigner) in front of his friends, at which everyone laughed, the Swiss man included. I couldn't believe it! For the first time, I had put myself on the firing line to satisfy someone else's craving for a particular dish. On the plus side, I now occupied the moral high ground. I had been selfless in the sacrifice of my dignity for the happiness of another and thought my Buddhist master would be proud of my spiritual development (even if I was still a self-confessed carnivore).

Since my "enlightening" crispy duck experience, I was actually enlightened once again, years later, to find that crispy aromatic duck is basically Chinese in origin and not something just concocted for foreigners, bearing a resemblance to tea-smoked Sichuan duck, Cantonese roast duck, and Peking duck. All four dishes use Chinese five spice, the difference being that crispy aromatic duck is deep-fried rather than oven-roasted. When I told my father this, he still maintained in his father-knows-best tone that "crispy duck is no good anyway because they fry the duck on its last days of freshness."

Crispy aromatic duck seems to be confined to the UK. The debate continues about who invented it. According to the previous generation of Chinese food lovers, the Richmond Rendezvous Group—a chain of restaurants that created the boom in Chinese cuisine in the mid-1960s—was responsible for this delicious recipe, which is consistently voted as the no. 1 Chinese takeout dish in Britain.

Peking duck is equally popular: Beijingers see it as the national dish of China, the crème de la crème of all dishes. Chefs are super-proud of the delicious smoky golden skin of the duck and tender, succulent flesh, achieved by first slathering the bird in a maltose glaze and air-drying for eight hours before filling with water and cooking it in a wood-fired oven so that the meat is steamed on the inside while the outside remains crisp. At a good restaurant, the waiter will meticulously carve the skin and meat in front of you and serve the skin with some fine sugar. This will be served with thin steamed pancakes made from wheat flour, sliced cucumber, scallions, and a good *tian mian jiang* (sweet flour sauce). You should also expect a good restaurant to ask you how you would like the rest of the duck cooked—either in a delicious herbal broth soup or in a stir-fry with lush greens (I usually go with the chef's recommendation). Both Peking duck and crispy duck are on my top list of favorite starters, so they are both included in this chapter, although my version of Peking duck is more like Cantonese roast duck because it is easier to re-create in the home kitchen.

I now have a tendency to judge dinner hosts based on their diplomacy when it comes to ordering (even if they are paying) and I am careful to be as sensitive as possible, to the point where I might be accused of being too nice. But better to be that, in my opinion, than greedy and selfish with no manners. There is a real art to ordering and being a good host; it takes real skill or *gong-fu* (kung fu). The Chinese are known for their generosity when it comes to dining, but a fine line needs to be trodden there as well: order too much and you look like a show-off; too little and you are seen as a scrooge. I take advice from my Buddhist master and that is: always finish what is on the table. It is better not to waste good food—think of all the people who go hungry.

When it comes to dinner parties at your own home, one thing is for sure: the very first dishes should impress. First impressions count. Like a teaser trailer to a blockbuster film, it should give you a hint of what to expect but without giving the whole plot away. It should excite and thrill you, satisfying you up to a point while leaving you hungry for more.

I usually serve a combination of "yang" dishes, "yang" being my label for "fried" because it doesn't sound so bad. Yes, we all know that fried food comes with an "unhealthy" tag, but it is all a matter of what you choose to eat. If you served and ate only fried food, you would soon be in the emergency room. Like everything in life, food choices are about balance. "Yang" is appropriate because, in food terms, it means "hot" energy, i.e., food that creates more "heat" within the body. The opposite of this is "yin" or cooling energy. It is not good for the body to be too "yang," as it puts stress on the body. So my "yang" menu carries this health warning—do not serve all these fried dishes in one meal; they are meant to be served only as an accompaniment to a variety of balanced dishes.

I have included many of my favorite naughty "yang" takeout starters (see pages 42–60), such as Pork and Shrimp Fried Wontons and Crispy Sweet Chili Beef Pancakes, my take on crispy duck pancakes. If this is all too "yang" for you, then fear not, as I have also included some "leng" starters, i.e., "cooling" dishes that are more balanced and not fried (see pages 61–73).

Vegetable spring rolls (chun juen)

Some may think this isn't a traditional Chinese dish—but it is, usually eaten at the Spring Festival or Chinese New Year. It has northern Chinese roots where wheat flour is the main form of carbohydrate and *bings*—semi-rolled pancakes—are eaten, with various delicious fillings wrapped inside.

PREP TIME: 20 minutes, plus 10 minutes for cooling
COOK IN: 7 minutes • **MAKES:** 12 small rolls

2½ cups peanut oil

1 tsp of peeled and grated fresh ginger

3½ oz shiitake mushrooms, sliced

3½ oz canned bamboo shoots, drained and cut into matchsticks

1½ tbsps of light soy sauce

1 tbsp of Chinese five-spice powder

3 oz bean sprouts

2 large scallions, sliced lengthwise

1 small carrot, cut into matchsticks

1 tbsp of vegetarian oyster sauce

Pinch of sea salt

Pinch of ground white pepper

24 small spring roll wrappers (6 inches square)

1 tbsp of cornstarch mixed with 1 tbsp of water

1. Heat a wok over high heat until it starts to smoke and then add 1 tbsp of the peanut oil. Add the ginger and stir-fry for a few seconds. Add the mushrooms and bamboo shoots and stir-fry for 1–2 minutes, then season with 1 tbsp of the soy sauce and the five-spice powder. Remove from the wok and set aside to cool for 10 minutes.

2. Put the bean sprouts, scallions, and carrot into a bowl, add the fried mushrooms and bamboo shoots, and season with the oyster sauce, remaining soy sauce, and the salt and pepper. Stir all the ingredients together to mix.

3. Take 2 spring roll wrappers and lay one on top of the other. (The extra layer will help prevent the skin from breaking.) Spoon 2 tbsps of filling into the center of the top wrapper and brush each corner with the cornstarch paste.

4. With the wrappers laid out in a diamond shape before you, bring the two side corners to meet in the middle, then bring the lower corner to the middle and roll the pastry with the filling toward the top corner. Tuck in the top edge and seal it with the cornstarch paste. Continue in the same way until all the wrappers are filled.

5. Place a wok over high heat and add the remaining peanut oil. Heat the oil to 350°F, or until a cube of bread dropped in turns golden brown in 15 seconds and floats to the surface. Deep-fry the spring rolls for about 5 minutes or until golden brown, then remove with a slotted spoon and drain on paper towels. Serve with a dipping sauce, such as sweet chili sauce, if you like.

> **CHING'S TIP**
> For a healthier "baked" option, substitute 5-inch squares of filo pastry for the spring roll wrappers. Brush one sheet with peanut oil, cover with a second sheet, and brush with oil again. Fill as in the recipe, then place on a baking sheet and bake in the oven (preheated to 350°F) for 20 minutes.

Crispy seaweed

This does not originate in China—it was invented by Chinese cooks in the West. It doesn't actually contain seaweed but is made with bok choy leaves that are finely shredded and deep-fried. I like to season mine with salt and granulated sugar so that it's sweet and salty. It's a great way to use up any bok choy you may have that is slightly past its best, and is also great as an appetizer or sprinkled as a garnish over crispy squid.

PREP TIME: 10 minutes • **COOK IN:** 2 minutes • **SERVES:** 2–4 to share

2½ cups peanut oil

7 oz bok choy leaves, finely shredded and stems removed

Sea salt and granulated sugar, for sprinkling

1 tsp of white sesame seeds, toasted (see the tip below)

1. Place a wok over high heat and pour in the peanut oil. Heat the oil to 350°F, or until a cube of bread dropped in turns golden brown in 15 seconds and floats to the surface.

2. Add half the bok choy leaves and deep-fry for a few seconds, then lift out using a slotted spoon and drain on paper towels. Deep-fry the remaining bok choy leaves and drain in the same way.

3. Season the "seaweed" with salt and sugar to taste, then transfer to a serving dish, sprinkle over the toasted sesame seeds, and serve immediately.

> **CHING'S TIP**
> You can buy sesame seeds pre-toasted, but they taste much better if you toast them yourself. Simply add the raw seeds to a skillet set over medium heat and dry-roast, tossing occasionally, for 1–2 minutes or until they begin to brown and become fragrant. Keep a close eye on them, as they can quickly burn, and remove from the heat as soon as they are toasted.
>
> **ALSO TRY**
> For a non-vegetarian option, you could sprinkle over dried pork or fish floss instead of the toasted sesame seeds.

Sesame shrimp toast

This dish is a takeout classic. Instead of grinding the shrimp, however, I keep them whole, wrapping them in whole wheat toast and sesame seeds and then frying them until golden brown. They are delicious served with sweet chili sauce.

PREP TIME: 15 minutes • **COOK IN:** 5 minutes • **MAKES:** 8 toasts

1 tsp of peeled and grated fresh ginger

1 large scallion, finely chopped

1 egg, beaten

1 tbsp of cornstarch

Dash of toasted sesame oil

Dash of light soy sauce

Salt and ground white pepper

½ cup of white sesame seeds, toasted (see the tip opposite)

4 slices of whole wheat toast, halved and crusts removed

8 raw tiger shrimp, shelled and deveined, tails left on

2½ cups peanut oil

1. Combine the ginger, scallion, beaten egg, cornstarch, toasted sesame oil, and soy sauce in a bowl and season with 2 pinches of salt and some white pepper. Place the sesame seeds in another bowl.

2. Dip a half piece of toast in the mixture and coat well. Then wrap the toast around a shrimp and squeeze slightly so that the bread fully covers the shrimp. Roll the wrapped shrimp in sesame seeds and coat well. Repeat with the remaining shrimp and pieces of toast.

3. Place a wok over high heat, add the peanut oil, and heat to 350°F, or until a cube of bread dropped in turns golden brown in 15 seconds and floats to the surface. Deep-fry the sesame shrimp toasts for 4–5 minutes or until golden brown, then remove with a slotted spoon, drain on paper towels, and serve immediately.

"Stinky"-style aromatic tofu with kimchi

Stinky tofu is made by fermenting tofu in a pungent brine, which gives it a distinctive smell and flavor. Traditionally, the brine consists of fermented milk, dried shrimp, mustard greens, bamboo shoots, and Chinese herbs. It does smell strong, but it is extremely flavorful. This dish is one of my favorite street-food snacks and I often have a craving for it. The tofu is deep-fried and served with sour cabbage and chili sauce. This is my own version. I like to marinate tofu that has been already fried (and which you can buy in a Chinese supermarket) in garlic, mirin, and five-spice powder, then deep-fry it and serve with some Korean-style kimchi and a good hot chili sauce.

PREP TIME: 10 minutes, plus 1 hour for marinating
COOK IN: 3 minutes • **SERVES:** 2–4 to share

Eight 2½-inch square pieces of deep-fried tofu
¼ cup potato flour or cornstarch
2½ cups peanut oil

FOR THE MARINADE
2 cloves of garlic, crushed and thinly sliced
¼ cup mirin
1 tbsp of clear rice vinegar or cider vinegar
1 tsp of Chinese five-spice powder

TO GARNISH (OPTIONAL)
Pinch of medium chili powder
Few sprigs of cilantro

TO SERVE (IN SEPARATE DISHES)
3 tbsps of kimchi
2 tbsps of chili bean sauce
2 tbsps of chili sauce mixed with 2 tbsps of oyster sauce
2 tbsps of hot chili sauce

1. Mix together all the ingredients for the marinade in a bowl and add the tofu pieces, then cover the bowl with plastic wrap and leave to marinate for 1 hour. Lift the tofu pieces out of the marinade, giving them a good squeeze to remove any excess liquid, then dust with the potato flour or cornstarch.

2. Place a wok over high heat and add the peanut oil. Heat the oil to 350°F, or until a piece of bread dropped in turns golden brown in 15 seconds and floats to the surface. Fry the tofu for 2–3 minutes or until golden and crisp on the outside, then drain on paper towels and cut into triangular wedges (each square cut in half, diagonally, to give 16 triangles).

3. Transfer to a serving plate and dust with the chili powder and sprinkle with the cilantro if you like. Serve with the assortment of small dishes of kimchi, chili bean sauce, chili oyster sauce, and hot chili sauce.

Sichuan salt and pepper squid

Squid contains lots of nutrients, including zinc, manganese, copper, selenium, and vitamin B12. When cooked well, it has a delicious soft, chewy texture. I was once fed squid sperm sacs stir-fried with egg and scallions in a seafood restaurant in Hong Kong and it certainly was an acquired taste! Squid itself is not so challenging, however, and salt and pepper squid is one of the most popular starters to be served in Chinese restaurants as well as appearing on some takeout menus. This dish is easy to make and does not require much effort. I love the numbing heat from the Sichuan peppercorns: just dry-toast them in a pan and grind them well to ensure the maximum flavor.

PREP TIME: 15 minutes • **COOK IN:** 5 minutes • **SERVES:** 2–4 to share

1 egg, beaten

3½ oz potato flour or cornstarch

2½ cups peanut oil

7 oz squid, cleaned and sliced into rings

Salt

2 pinches of dried chili flakes

1 tbsp of Sichuan peppercorns, toasted and ground (see the tip below)

TO SERVE

Lemon wedges

Fruity Chili Sauce (see page 57)

Sprigs of cilantro

1. Mix the beaten egg with the potato flour or cornstarch and 2 tbsps of water to make a batter.

2. Heat a large wok over high heat and add the peanut oil. Heat the oil to 350°F, or until a cube of bread dropped in turns golden brown in 15 seconds and floats to the surface.

3. Dip the squid rings into the batter and carefully drop into the hot oil. Deep-fry for 4–5 minutes or until golden, then lift out using a slotted spoon and drain on paper towels. Season with a little salt, the dried chili flakes, and ground toasted Sichuan peppercorns, then serve with lemon wedges and the Fruity Chili Sauce and garnish with cilantro sprigs.

> **CHING'S TIP**
> To toast the Sichuan peppercorns, heat a small wok or saucepan over medium heat, then add the peppercorns and dry-roast for 1 minute, or until fragrant. Transfer to a spice grinder or mortar and pestle and grind to a powder. Alternatively, place in a plastic bag and smash with a rolling pin.

Five-spice salted shrimp with hot cilantro sauce

This is my take on salt and pepper shrimp: shrimp coated in a starchy batter and deep-fried, then tossed in a spicy salt and served with a grapefruit and cilantro dipping sauce. It also makes a sophisticated appetizer for serving with cocktails.

PREP TIME: 10 minutes • **COOK IN:** 5 minutes • **SERVES:** 2–4 to share

1 egg, beaten

3½ oz potato flour or cornstarch

2½ cups peanut oil

12 raw tiger shrimp, shelled and deveined, tails left on

FOR THE GRAPEFRUIT AND CILANTRO SAUCE

1 tbsp of peeled and grated fresh ginger

1 green chili, sliced

1 red chili, sliced

2 tbsps of lemon juice

Juice of ½ large pink grapefruit (pulp included)

Handful of cilantro leaves, finely chopped

FOR THE SPICE MIX

1 tsp of Chinese five-spice powder

1 tsp of sea salt

1 tsp of ground white pepper

1. Mix together all the ingredients for the sauce in a bowl and set aside. In a separate bowl, mix together the egg, potato flour or cornstarch, and 2 tbsps of water to make a batter. Set aside.

2. Place a wok over high heat, add the peanut oil, and heat to 350°F, or until a cube of bread dropped in turns golden brown in 15 seconds and floats to the surface.

3. Dip each shrimp in the batter and then lower into the oil, one at a time. Cook for 4–5 minutes, or until the shrimp turn golden, and then remove from the oil with a slotted spoon and drain on paper towels. Mix together the ingredients for the spice mix and sprinkle over the cooked shrimp, toss well, and eat immediately, served with the cilantro sauce.

Japanese-style crispy halibut with lemon sauce

If you enjoy ordering lemon chicken from your local takeout shop, then you will like this dish. It rather resembles English-style fish fingers—without the lemon sauce, that is! I like to use a good white-fleshed fish; cod is overfished, hence I've used halibut here, but pollack would do just as well. You could even use mackerel if you wished. I like using the Japanese panko breadcrumbs because they have been flavored with honey and are extra crisp, but you could make your own breadcrumbs, of course, using a chunk of stale bread. The dipping sauce is easy to make too.

PREP TIME: 15 minutes • **COOK IN:** 5 minutes • **SERVES:** 2–4 to share

7 oz halibut fillet, cut into ½-inch strips

Sea salt and ground white pepper

3½ oz potato flour or cornstarch

1 egg, beaten

5 oz panko breadcrumbs

2½ cups peanut oil

Dried chili flakes (optional)

Lemon wedges, to garnish (optional)

FOR THE SAUCE

1 tbsp of peeled and grated fresh ginger

1 tbsp of light soy sauce

1 tbsp of honey

1 tbsp of Shaohsing rice wine or dry sherry

7 tbsps of cold vegetable stock

¼ cup lemon juice

1 tbsp of cornstarch

1. Season the halibut pieces with salt and white pepper. Put the potato flour or cornstarch, beaten egg, and breadcrumbs in three separate bowls. Dip the halibut pieces into the potato flour or cornstarch, then the egg, and coat in the breadcrumbs.

2. Place a wok over high heat and add all but 1 tbsp of the peanut oil. Heat the oil to 350°F, or until a piece of bread dropped in turns golden brown in 15 seconds and floats to the surface. Fry the breaded halibut pieces in the oil for 3–4 minutes or until golden brown, then remove with a slotted spoon and drain on paper towels.

3. Meanwhile, make the sauce. Heat a small wok or saucepan over medium heat and add the remaining 1 tbsp of peanut oil. Add the ginger and fry for a few seconds, then add the remaining ingredients and bring to a boil. Cook for 1 minute or until the sauce has thickened, then remove from the heat.

4. When the fish is cooked, season with dried chili flakes (if using), garnish with lemon wedges, if you like, and serve with the lemon dipping sauce.

Chinese-style soft-shell crabs

In Chinese cooking, crabs are served in a variety of ways, from steamed and braised to deep-fried. This is a popular dish, served in Chinese restaurants all over the world. It's also one of my favorite dishes.

Soft-shell crabs can be bought in the frozen section of a Chinese supermarket. The most well-known variety is the blue crab from America. As the crabs grow, they molt their old shells and for a short period between May and July their new shell remains soft and delicate.

PREP TIME: 15 minutes, plus 20 minutes for marinating
COOK IN: 4 minutes • **SERVES:** 2–4 to share

4 frozen small soft-shell crabs, defrosted

2 eggs, beaten

7 oz potato flour or cornstarch

2½ cups peanut oil

2 large pinches of sea salt

2 large pinches of ground black pepper

1 tsp of dried chili flakes

FOR THE MARINADE

1 tbsp of peanut oil

1 tbsp of peeled and grated fresh ginger

1 tsp of Shaohsing rice wine or dry sherry

1 tsp of Chinese five-spice powder

¼ tsp of medium chili powder

1 tbsp of clear rice vinegar or cider vinegar

TO GARNISH

2 scallions, thinly sliced

2 red chilies, seeded (optional) and sliced

1. To prepare a crab, first cut away the face (this can taste bitter), slicing behind the eyes. Next, lift the flap on the underside of the crab and cut this off. Loosen the top "shell" of the body and lift it up to reveal the gills (plume-like filaments also known as "dead man's fingers"—there are eight on each side of the crab's body). These are inedible and should be removed, along with any brown meat. Rinse the crab well and prepare the remaining crabs in the same way.

2. Mix together all the marinade ingredients in a bowl, then add the crabs, cover with plastic wrap, and leave to marinate for 20 minutes. In a separate bowl, mix together the eggs, potato flour or cornstarch, and 2 tbsps of water to make a batter.

3. Place a wok over high heat and add the peanut oil. Heat the oil to 350°F, or until a cube of bread dropped in turns golden brown in 15 seconds and floats to the surface.

4. Remove the crabs from the marinade and drain. Dip the crabs in the batter and then gently lower into the hot oil using a slotted spoon. Deep-fry for 3–4 minutes, or until golden, and then remove and drain on paper towels. Season with the salt, pepper, and chili flakes, then garnish with the scallions and red chilies and serve immediately.

Sweet-and-sour Wuxi ribs

This dish originates from Wuxi in Zhejiang province. As this borders the neighboring Shanghai municipality, it means that the dish can be found in many Shanghai restaurants too. The traditional way of preparing the ribs is to braise them slowly in stock for an hour, then add the sauce.

PREP TIME: 15 minutes, plus 20 minutes for marinating
COOK IN: 10 minutes • **SERVES:** 2–4 to share

1 lb 5 oz pork ribs, chopped into 1¼- to 1½-inch pieces

1⅔ cups peanut oil

Sea salt and ground white pepper

1 scallion, thinly sliced, to garnish

FOR THE MARINADE

2 cloves of garlic, finely chopped

2 tbsps of yellow bean sauce

1 tbsp of Shaohsing rice wine or dry sherry

FOR THE SWEET-AND-SOUR SAUCE

2 tbsps of light soy sauce

2 tbsps of Chinkiang black rice vinegar or balsamic vinegar

1 tbsp of light brown sugar

1 tbsp of honey

1. Put all the ingredients for the marinade into a large bowl and stir to combine. Add the pork ribs and turn to coat, then cover the bowl with plastic wrap and leave to marinate for at least 20 minutes in the fridge.

2. Place a wok over high heat and add the peanut oil. Heat the oil to 350°F, or until a cube of bread dropped in turns golden brown in 15 seconds and floats to the surface. Using a slotted spoon, carefully add the ribs and fry for 4–5 minutes, or until browned and cooked through. Lift the ribs out of the wok and drain on paper towels.

3. While the ribs are cooking, place all the ingredients for the sweet-and-sour sauce in a small bowl and stir to combine.

4. Drain the wok of oil and wipe it clean, then place back over high heat. Add the ribs and sauce mixture to the wok and cook over medium-to-low heat for 5–6 minutes, or until the sauce has reduced to a sticky consistency. Season to taste with salt and pepper, garnish with the scallion, and serve immediately.

Crispy sweet chili beef pancakes

This is just like crispy duck pancakes but using beef instead of duck. The beef is coated in batter and then fried until crisp. To make a quick and easy sweet sauce, I have used a mixture of light soy, orange juice, and store-bought sweet chili sauce.

PREP TIME: 20 minutes • **COOK IN:** 10 minutes • **SERVES:** 2–4 to share

11 oz beef sirloin, fat removed, very thinly sliced

2 tbsps of cornstarch

2½ cups peanut oil

FOR THE FRUITY CHILI SAUCE

2 tbsps of light soy sauce

2 tbsps of sweet chili sauce

Juice of 1 small orange

TO SERVE

2 carrots, cut into matchsticks

½ cucumber (unpeeled), cut into matchsticks

2 scallions, thinly sliced lengthwise

12 small wheat-flour pancakes

ALSO TRY
If you like, you could turn this dish into crispy beef by adding fried beef pieces to the thickened sauce in the wok, tossing together and garnishing with orange zest.

1. Prepare all the vegetables for serving, place them on a plate, cover with plastic wrap, and refrigerate.

2. Place the pancakes in a small bamboo steamer set over a saucepan of boiling water (making sure the bottom of the steamer doesn't touch the water) and steam for 5 minutes. Reduce the heat to low and keep the pancakes warm in the steamer until ready to serve.

3. Dip the beef strips in the cornstarch, shaking off any excess flour, then place on a plate. Set a wok over high heat and add the peanut oil. Heat the oil to 350°F, or until a cube of bread dropped in turns golden brown in 15 seconds and floats to the surface. Deep-fry the beef for 4–5 minutes or until golden, then drain on paper towels.

4. While the beef is draining, place a small wok or skillet over high heat, add all the ingredients for the sauce, and allow to bubble away until thickened.

5. Place the cooked beef on a serving plate and set on the table with the vegetables, warm sauce, and pancakes, so that everyone can help themselves. To assemble a pancake, smear over some of the sauce, add a few strips of carrot, cucumber, and scallion, followed by a few pieces of crispy beef, then roll up and eat.

Pork and shrimp fried wontons

These delicious wontons are deep-fried until golden and dipped in sweet-and-sour chili sauce. This is a popular starter and you can vary the filling, using pork and Chinese mushrooms, pork and water chestnuts, or shrimp and chives—the possibilities are endless.

PREP TIME: 20 minutes • **COOK IN:** 7 minutes • **SERVES:** 4

28 wonton wrappers
  (3 inches square)
1 egg, beaten
2½ cups peanut oil

FOR THE FILLING

7 oz ground pork

3½ oz raw shelled and
  deveined freshwater shrimp
  or tiger shrimp, roughly
  chopped

1 large scallion, finely
  chopped

3 shiitake mushrooms, finely
  diced

1 tbsp of peeled and grated
  fresh ginger

1 tbsp of Shaohsing rice wine
  or dry sherry

1 tbsp of cornstarch

Pinch of sea salt

Pinch of ground white pepper

1. Place all the ingredients for the filling in a bowl and mix well.

2. To prevent the wrappers from opening up and separating from the filling once cooked, brush the inside of each with the beaten egg. Take one wrapper and place a small teaspoon of the filling in the center. Gather up the sides of the wrapper and mold around the filling into a ball shape, twisting the top to secure it. Repeat with the remaining wrappers, filling and molding them in the same way.

3. Place a wok over high heat and add the peanut oil. Heat the oil to 350°F, or until a cube of bread dropped in turns golden brown in 15 seconds and floats to the surface. Deep-fry half the wontons for about 3 minutes or until golden, then remove with a slotted spoon and drain on paper towels. Repeat with the remaining wontons, then serve with the Fruity Chili Sauce from page 57, if you like.

Fried sweet chili chicken skewers

In the spirit of Westernized Chinese takeout dishes, I have to admit this is my own contribution. It is naughty but very, very good—even if I do say so myself.

PREP TIME: 15 minutes • **COOK IN:** 10 minutes • **SERVES:** 2–4 to share

3 large chicken thighs, skin on, boned and halved

Sea salt and ground white pepper

¼ cup cornstarch

2 egg whites

2½ cups peanut oil

Small handful of chopped cilantro

FOR THE SAUCE

3 cloves of garlic, finely chopped

1-inch piece of fresh ginger, peeled and sliced

1 red chili, seeded and finely chopped

6 tbsps of sweet chili sauce

1 tbsp of light soy sauce

Juice of 1 lime

SIX 3-INCH BAMBOO SKEWERS (PRE-SOAKED IN WATER FOR 20 MINUTES TO PREVENT BURNING)

1. Thread each chicken piece onto a skewer, then season with salt and pepper. Place the cornstarch and egg whites in a bowl and mix to make a batter.

2. Place a wok over high heat and add the peanut oil. Heat the oil to 350°F, or until a cube of bread dropped in turns golden brown in 15 seconds and floats to the surface.

3. Dip the chicken skewers in the batter, then lower into the oil and deep-fry for about 5 minutes, or until crisp and golden. Lift out using tongs or a slotted spoon and drain on paper towels. Pour the oil from the wok through a sieve into a heatproof container.

4. To make the sauce, wipe out the wok and place back over high heat. Add 1 tbsp of the drained oil, and when it starts to smoke, add the garlic, ginger, and chili and stir-fry for a few seconds, then add the remaining ingredients and mix well.

5. Return the cooked chicken to the wok and turn to coat in the hot sauce, then stir in the cilantro and serve immediately.

Celery and tofu gan salad with sesame dressing

Tofu gan is dried firm bean curd or tofu that has virtually no moisture in it, unlike fresh bean curd. It is often stewed with soy sauce and lashings of Chinese five spice and sugar. It is then drained, sliced, and stir-fried, in true Sichuan fashion, with garlic, leeks, dried chilies, and scallions in a spiced chili oil. I also like tofu gan sliced and served with *lu-dan* (hard-boiled eggs also stewed in the same mixture of soy sauce and spices). In some Chinese supermarkets you can buy prepared tofu gan in vacuum packs, which you can then slice and make into this delicious chilled salad.

PREP TIME: 5 minutes, plus 30 minutes for chilling • **SERVES:** 2–4 to share

2 stalks of celery, cut on the diagonal into ¼-inch slices

4 pieces of tofu gan (dried firm bean curd), sliced

Small handful of finely chopped cilantro

FOR THE DRESSING

1 tsp of peeled and grated fresh ginger

½ tsp of chili bean paste

1 tbsp of peanut oil

1 tbsp of clear rice vinegar or cider vinegar

1 tbsp of mirin

1 tbsp of toasted sesame oil

Whisk together all the ingredients for the dressing in a bowl, add the celery and tofu gan pieces, and turn in the dressing to coat. Cover with plastic wrap and place in the fridge to chill for 30 minutes. Serve garnished with the chopped cilantro.

Sesame green beans

Greens beans are delicious in any dish, whether eaten cold in salads or hot in stir-fries. They are at their very best in the middle of summer. When choosing green beans, go for ones that snap easily and have a smooth, green, unblemished skin. They have a mild, fresh sweet flavor and are best cooked at a high temperature until crisp to lock in their color and flavor. In China, they have a type of very long green bean known as a snake bean. These are usually deep-fried and then stir-fried so that they are tender and full of flavor. You can use snake beans in this recipe too, if you can get hold of them. This is a simple, quick recipe that can be served cold or hot, either as an appetizer or as an accompaniment to a main dish.

PREP TIME: 5 minutes, plus 30 minutes for chilling (if serving cold)
COOK IN: 2 minutes • **SERVES:** 2–4 to share

Salt

5 oz green beans, topped and tailed, then chopped into 1½-inch lengths

Black and white sesame seeds, toasted (see the tip on page 44), for sprinkling

FOR THE DRESSING

1 clove of garlic, crushed

2 tbsps of mirin

2 tbsps of light soy sauce

2 tbsps of clear rice vinegar or cider vinegar

2 tbsps of toasted sesame oil

1. Place the ingredients for the dressing in a bowl and mix well.

2. Bring a saucepan of salted water to a boil, add the beans, and blanch for 2 minutes, then remove and drain.

3. If serving hot, transfer the beans to a bowl and toss in the dressing, then sprinkle over the toasted sesame seeds and serve immediately. If serving cold, rinse the warm beans in cold running water and drain well. Place in a dish, coat in the dressing, and then cover with plastic wrap and chill in the fridge for 30 minutes. Sprinkle over the toasted sesame seeds just before serving.

Plums and heirloom tomatoes with sweet basil and salted plum shavings

This is a summer recipe at its best: great served as a starter to a Chinese-themed barbecue. Juicy heirloom tomatoes are delicious and full of flavor, although large ripe beefsteak tomatoes would do instead. Couple these with plums and sweet basil leaves and you have my twist on the Italian caprese salad. What gives this dish extra punch is the sweet-sour shavings of Chinese preserved salted plum sprinkled over the top. If you have some Asian pears, you can peel them and add slices in between the tomatoes and plums to give a different texture.

PREP TIME: 10 minutes • **SERVES:** 4 to share

4 large ripe heirloom tomatoes or beefsteak tomatoes, sliced

6 plums, peeled and pits removed, then sliced

2 Asian pears, peeled, cored, and sliced (optional)

Handful of Thai or Italian sweet basil leaves

Pinch of sea salt

1 preserved salted plum, grated

FOR THE DRESSING

3 tbsps of extra-virgin olive oil

3 tbsps of aged balsamic vinegar

1. Arrange the tomatoes, plums, pears (if using), and basil leaves in alternating layers on a serving plate.

2. Mix together the ingredients for the dressing and pour over the salad just before serving, sprinkling over the salt and the salted plum shavings to finish.

Pickled whole radishes with cilantro

I am a big fan of radishes, of whatever kind. They come in a variety of shapes and colors, including the white Chinese radish, or daikon. Having lived in the West for most of my life, I have grown to love red radishes and look forward to them every spring and summer. My favorite are the French breakfast radishes—long red and white roots like my two-tone Topshop Mary Jane shoes. This is one of my favorite pickled recipes—quick and easy and full of flavor, to get the taste buds going.

PREP TIME: 5 minutes, plus 1 hour for marinating • **SERVES:** 2–4 to share

12 radishes (preferably French breakfast), tops trimmed

Small handful of cilantro, finely chopped, to garnish

FOR THE PICKLING LIQUID

3 tbsps of mirin

3 tbsps of clear rice vinegar or cider vinegar

1 tbsp of light soy sauce

½ tsp of superfine sugar

Pinch of salt

Mix together all the ingredients for the pickling liquid in a shallow bowl. Drown the radishes in this, then cover with plastic wrap, place in the fridge, and leave to marinate for 1 hour. Serve sprinkled with the finely chopped cilantro.

Cold sesame shrimp and cucumber

For this dish, it really pays to use the sweetest cucumbers you can get your hands on: choose ones that are weighty and have a smooth, unwrinkled skin. I like using young tender small cucumbers if I can, as you don't need to seed them and they add extra sweetness and crunch. This recipe makes the perfect summer appetizer, or it can be served as a lunch for two on a bed of watercress leaves and sliced yellow peppers. The dressing is quite delicious too.

PREP TIME: 5 minutes, plus 30 minutes for chilling • **SERVES:** 2–4 to share

5 oz cooked shelled and deveined tiger shrimp

½ cucumber (unpeeled), halved lengthwise and cut into ¼-inch slices

Black and white sesame seeds, toasted (see the tip on page 44), for sprinkling

5–6 chives, finely chopped, to garnish

FOR THE DRESSING

2 tbsps of mirin

2 tbsps of light soy sauce

2 tbsps of clear rice vinegar or cider vinegar

2 tbsps of toasted sesame oil

1. Place the shrimp and cucumber slices in a serving bowl and mix together. Pour the ingredients for the dressing into another bowl and stir to combine, then add to the shrimp and cucumbers and mix well. Cover with plastic wrap, transfer to the fridge, and chill for 30 minutes.

2. Just before serving, sprinkle over the toasted sesame seeds and garnish with the finely chopped chives.

Chili crayfish tails and mango lettuce wraps

Some may think that crayfish tails are not a Chinese ingredient, but in fact China is the largest producer of crayfish in the world. Spicy Sichuan crayfish is a very popular restaurant dish, delicious washed down with a glass of cold beer. In the UK, supermarkets stock cooked crayfish tails preserved in brine. I love the flavor of crayfish tails; they are a real treat and make a change to shrimp. This is one of my quick and easy "fu-sian" starters, refreshing but with a hint of chili, and great to make for a summer barbecue to serve with a variety of dishes.

PREP TIME: 10 minutes • **SERVES:** 2–4 to share

3½ oz cooked crayfish tails in brine, drained

1 ripe mango, peeled and pit removed, then diced

8 sugar snap peas, sliced lengthwise

Small handful of cilantro, finely chopped, plus extra to garnish (optional)

1 red chili, seeded and finely chopped

Boston lettuce leaves, to serve

FOR THE SAUCE

3 tbsps of sweet chili sauce

1 tbsp of fish sauce (nam pla)

1 tbsp of freshly squeezed lime juice

1 tbsp of freshly squeezed grapefruit juice

1 tbsp of extra-virgin olive oil

1. In a bowl, whisk together the ingredients for the sauce and set aside.

2. Place the crayfish tails in a serving dish and mix together with the mango, sugar snap peas, cilantro (if using), and chili.

3. Just before eating, spoon the sauce over the crayfish mixture and stir to combine. Garnish with a cilantro sprig, if you like, and place on the table with a bowl of lettuce leaves for people to help themselves. To assemble the dish, take a spoonful of the crayfish mixture, place in the middle of a lettuce leaf, and eat immediately.

Cantonese-style roast duck and cucumber slices with salt and pepper

I am used to being served cold meats for a starter in a Chinese restaurant, such as beef shin in Sichuan spicy oil, cold roast Cantonese-style pork, or cold chicken's feet. So I decided to make my own version of Cantonese-style roast duck, served cold with cucumber slices. A light, healthy dish, this can be easily prepared in advance for a dinner party and tastes delicious served with a glass of Riesling.

PREP TIME: 10 minutes, plus 30 minutes for cooling/chilling
COOK IN: 10 minutes • **SERVES:** 4 to share

Two 9-oz duck breasts, skin on
1 tbsp of Shaohsing rice wine or dry sherry
½ tsp of sea salt
2 tsps of Chinese five-spice powder
Sprig of cilantro, to garnish (optional)

TO SERVE
1 cucumber (unpeeled), halved lengthwise, seeded, and thinly sliced
2 scallions, thinly sliced

FOR THE SALT AND PEPPER MIX
1 tbsp of cracked sea salt
1 tbsp of ground white pepper

1. Preheat the oven to 425°F.

2. Pierce the skin of the duck breasts with a fork, then pour over some boiling water and pat the skin dry with paper towels. The hot water helps to release some of the fat and ensure that the skin is crisp when cooked.

3. Place the duck breasts in a roasting pan, add the rice wine or dry sherry, and season on both sides with the salt and Chinese five-spice powder. Roast for 10 minutes and then remove from the oven and leave to cool for a few minutes.

4. Once the duck has cooled down, cover with plastic wrap and place in the fridge to chill for 20 minutes. To serve, slice and arrange on a serving plate, alternating with slices of cucumber and sprinkled with the thinly sliced scallions. Garnish with cilantro sprigs, if you like. Mix together the cracked sea salt and white pepper in a small bowl and serve with the duck for dipping.

Cantonese-style roast duck with mango salad and plum dressing

This is a recipe I created when I was running my food kitchen in East London, although sadly it was never used because mangoes are quite expensive. It has now been resurrected and I proudly share it here. It makes a delectable starter, or for those watching their waistlines, it can also be served as a light supper.

PREP TIME: 10 minutes, plus 30 minutes for cooling/chilling
COOK IN: 10 minutes • **SERVES:** 2–4 to share

Two 9-oz duck breasts, skin on

1 tbsp of Shaohsing rice wine or dry sherry

½ tsp of sea salt

2 tsps of Chinese five-spice powder

FOR THE PLUM DRESSING

2 tbsps of plum sauce

2 tbsps of light soy sauce

2 tbsps of extra-virgin olive oil

4 tbsps of freshly squeezed orange juice

FOR THE SALAD

3½ oz mixed salad leaves (such as watercress, baby spinach, and arugula)

½ cucumber (unpeeled), halved lengthwise and cut into ¼-inch slices

2 scallions, sliced lengthwise

8 snow peas, thinly sliced ⅛ inch thick lengthwise

1 ripe mango, peeled and pit removed, then sliced

1. For cooking and chilling the duck breasts, follow the instructions for Cantonese-Style Roast Duck and Cucumber Slices with Salt and Pepper on page 68.

2. Meanwhile, whisk together all the ingredients for the plum dressing. Remove the duck from the fridge and cut into slices.

3. To assemble the dish, arrange the salad leaves, cucumber, scallions, and snow peas on a serving plate, place the sliced duck breast on top, then decorate with the mango slices, drizzle over a little of the dressing, and serve.

> **ALSO TRY**
> If you like the texture of glass noodles, you could add pre-soaked ones to this dish and serve it as a refreshing noodle salad.

Mu shu pork

This dish originates from northern China. It traditionally consists of stir-fried pork and Chinese cabbage, all finely chopped so that they can be served stuffed in steamed wheat-flour pancakes or buns. I have decided to vary the dish and, instead of the cabbage, use a tasty mixture of crunchy bamboo shoots, Chinese wood ear mushrooms, and dry-roasted peanuts.

PREP TIME: 20 minutes • **COOK IN:** 10 minutes • **SERVES:** 4 to share

12 small wheat-flour pancakes

2 tbsps of peanut oil

2 cloves of garlic, crushed and finely chopped

1 tbsp of peeled and grated fresh ginger

2 dried Chinese mushrooms, soaked in hot water for 20 minutes, then drained and finely diced, or 2 shiitake mushrooms, sliced

1 small carrot, diced

9 oz pork tenderloin, diced

1 tbsp of Shaohsing rice wine or dry sherry

2 oz preserved mustard greens or gherkins, finely diced (or use diced zucchini for a similar texture)

2 oz dried Chinese wood ear mushrooms, soaked in hot water for 20 minutes, drained, and finely chopped

4½ oz canned bamboo shoots, drained and diced

Handful of dry-roasted peanuts

2 tbsps of light soy sauce

1 tsp of toasted sesame oil

2–3 pinches of ground white pepper

1. Place the pancakes in a small bamboo steamer set over a saucepan of boiling water (making sure the bottom of the steamer doesn't touch the water) and steam for 5 minutes. Reduce the heat to low and keep the pancakes warm in the steamer until ready to serve.

2. Heat a wok over medium heat until it starts to smoke and then add the peanut oil. Add the garlic, ginger, Chinese or shiitake mushrooms, and carrot and stir-fry together for just under a minute.

3. Add the pork and cook for 2–3 minutes, or until it starts to turn brown, then stir in the rice wine or dry sherry.

4. Add the preserved mustard greens or gherkins, wood ear mushrooms, bamboo shoots, and peanuts and mix well together. Finally, season with the soy sauce, toasted sesame oil, and ground white pepper and serve wrapped in the steamed pancakes.

> **ALSO TRY**
> As an alternative to wheat-flour pancakes, use iceberg lettuce instead: carefully peel away the leaves and use them as "wraps," as served in Chinese takeout shops and restaurants.

Chicken &
Duck

When I stayed with my grandmother one summer in Taiwan, I witnessed her killing a live chicken. She did it ever so gently, making a small incision at the neck and draining the bird of its blood. I watched as the chicken's life swiftly ebbed away.

My grandmother collected the blood to make *ji xie gao* (literally "chicken's blood cake"), in which the blood is mixed with pre-cooked glutinous rice and then molded into rice cakes and grilled or wok-fried. It is a popular street snack. It also reflects a time when nothing of the bird was wasted—even its blood.

If only people were more in tune with their food today, as my grandparents were. I am a more thoughtful cook now; I always buy free-range or organic produce, I eat less meat, and am very careful not to waste anything.

With the chicken offal, my grandmother would make a broth using the heart and kidneys, cooked with ginger and rice wine. Sometimes she would make an herbal soup; at other times she would blanch the offal and then steam it and serve it chopped up with a dressing of oil, ginger, chili, and scallion. If there was any left over, she might then turn it into another dish by stir-frying it with leafy greens. Nothing was wasted and the whole bird would be eaten, even if it was through a few recycled meals. It didn't hurt us; the food always tasted delicious and was expertly prepared by an experienced cook.

The first time I witnessed the death of a chicken by my grandmother's hand, I couldn't quite bring myself to eat it. I had seen my uncle kill fish, so it should have been no different. But to see a chicken killed before my very eyes was a shock to the system. To liven my mood, my grandmother told me how, when my father and mother first got married, it was customary for the man to kill a chicken, to show his ability to look after his family. She said my father was useless at it. He had the whole family chasing after a headless chicken in the courtyard at his new in-laws' and was called a "fake" farmer's son after that! When I confronted my father with the story, he said that the bird had been so strong, his hands had slipped and it escaped from his grip. Needless to say, his new bride was highly embarrassed and his father-in-law singularly unimpressed. I wasn't surprised that my father had never mentioned that incident!

My grandmother always gave thanks to the animals that sacrificed their lives for us and every month at the time of the full moon she would give up eating meat as a sign of respect. The way she lived—peacefully and gracefully, with respect for nature and the environment—inspires me so much. These are the principles that influence the way I live and eat today.

It is mostly chicken that features in the recipes in this section, reflecting the meat's popularity in Chinese takeout. Takeout chicken is normally coated in a batter of egg white and cornstarch, a process known as velveting. The chicken is then fried in oil and drained before being used in such favorites as General Tso's Chicken and Kung Po Chicken (see pages 80 and 82). This technique keeps the meat lovely and tender and seals in all the juices. It is especially useful if you're cooking chicken breast, although I prefer to use thighs wherever possible because the meat is a lot juicier and more flavorful.

My tip is to season the chicken with salt and ground white pepper and then dust it lightly with potato flour or cornstarch before stir-frying it. Like velveting, this helps to seal in the juices but without having to fry the meat, therefore keeping the dish healthier. This flour coating can sometimes catch on the side of the wok, but don't worry if it does—just keep stirring and tossing the chicken. You can cook the chicken pieces first before adding to the dish. It can also be helpful to add a dash of water to help the chicken move around in the wok.

Yellow bean chicken with green beans and shiitake mushrooms

Served with boiled jasmine rice, this makes a quick and delicious as well as highly nutritious supper.

PREP TIME: 10 minutes, plus 20 minutes for marinating
COOK IN: 10 minutes • **SERVES:** 2–4 to share

1 lb skinless chicken breasts or thighs, sliced

2 tbsps of potato flour or cornstarch

1 tbsp of peanut oil

6½ oz green beans, topped and tailed, then chopped into 1½-inch pieces

4 shiitake mushrooms, stems removed, then sliced

Salt and freshly ground pepper (optional)

2 small scallions, finely chopped, to garnish

FOR THE MARINADE

2 cloves of garlic, crushed

1 tbsp of Shaohsing rice wine or dry sherry

1 tbsp of yellow bean paste

2 tbsps of light soy sauce

1 tbsp of honey

1. Mix together the ingredients for the marinade in a bowl, then add the chicken, turning it to coat in the mixture. Cover with plastic wrap and leave to marinate for 20 minutes, then remove from the marinade and coat in the potato flour or cornstarch.

2. Heat a wok over high heat until the wok starts to smoke and then add the peanut oil. Add the chicken and stir-fry for 4 minutes, then add the green beans and stir for 1 minute. Add the mushrooms and keep stirring for an additional 1–2 minutes.

3. Check the seasoning, seasoning further to taste, if needed. Sprinkle over the scallions, then remove from the heat and serve immediately.

Chicken and black bean stir-fry

I adore fermented black beans and this is one of my favorite easy suppers. I add a touch of a good-quality yellow bean sauce for a savory, mellow edge to the dish.

PREP TIME: 10 minutes • **COOK IN:** 5 minutes • **SERVES:** 2–4 to share

1 tbsp of peanut oil

5 cloves of garlic, finely chopped

1 tbsp of peeled and grated fresh ginger

1 red chili, seeded and chopped

1 bird's eye chili, seeded and chopped

1 tbsp of fermented salted black beans, rinsed and crushed

1 lb skinless chicken breasts or thighs, cut into ½-inch slices

1 tbsp of Shaohsing rice wine or dry sherry

2 green peppers, seeded and cut into chunks

1 scant cup vegetable stock

1 tbsp of light soy sauce

1 tbsp of cornstarch mixed with 2 tbsps of water

1. Heat a wok over high heat until it starts to smoke and then add the peanut oil. Add the garlic, ginger, and chilies and stir-fry for a few seconds, then add the fermented black beans and stir quickly.

2. Add the chicken slices and stir-fry for 1 minute, keeping the ingredients moving in the wok. As the meat starts to turn opaque, add the rice wine or dry sherry.

3. Add the green peppers and stir-fry for 1 minute, then add the stock and bring to a boil. Season with the soy sauce, then add the cornstarch paste and stir to thicken. Serve immediately with jasmine rice.

General Tso's chicken

There are many variations of this recipe all over the world and it is particularly popular as a takeout dish in America. Its inventor was from Hunan, a chef named Peng-Chang Kuei who fled with the Nationalist Party to Taiwan during the Second World War. Cooking for state banquets and official events for the Nationalist Party, he first came up with the dish in the 1950s, calling it after a Hunanese general from the Qing dynasty. Its original flavors were typically Hunanese—hot, sour, salty, and heavy—but when he moved to New York in 1973, he adapted the recipe for the American palate. Peng was a friend of Henry Kissinger and it was he who is believed to have popularized Hunan cuisine in America. The dish's popularity has spread back to China where, ironically, Hunan chefs now claim it as a speciality of the region!

The taste should be sweet and spicy with a slight zing from the chilies—Sichuan sun-dried chilies if you can find them. You might be surprised by the use of ketchup; you can also use tomato purée if you prefer, adding a tiny bit of sugar.

PREP TIME: 5 minutes • **COOK IN:** 9 minutes • **SERVES:** 2–4 to share

2 skinless chicken breasts or 4 thighs, cut into ½-inch cubes

Salt and ground white pepper

1 tbsp of potato flour or cornstarch

1 tbsp of peanut oil

1 clove of garlic, crushed

4 dried red chilies

1 tbsp of Shaohsing rice wine or dry sherry

4 scallions, chopped into 1-inch lengths

FOR THE SAUCE

1 tbsp of yellow bean sauce

1 tbsp of light soy sauce

1 tbsp of tomato ketchup

1 tbsp of chili sauce

1 tsp of light brown sugar or honey

1 tsp of dark soy sauce

1. Place the chicken in a bowl and season with salt and pepper. Add the potato flour or cornstarch and mix well. Place the ingredients for the sauce in another bowl and stir together.

2. Heat a wok over high heat until it starts to smoke and then add the peanut oil. Add the garlic and dried chilies and fry for a few seconds, then add the chicken pieces and stir-fry for 2 minutes. As the chicken starts to turn opaque, add the rice wine or dry sherry. Cook for another 2 minutes, then pour in the sauce and bring to a boil.

3. Cook the chicken in the sauce for an additional 2 minutes, or until it is cooked through and the sauce has reduced and thickened and is slightly sticky. Add the scallions and cook for just under 1 minute, then transfer to a serving plate and serve immediately.

Kung Po chicken

This is a classic dish from Sichuan. It is named after Ding Baochen (1820–86), a governor of Sichuan; "Gong Bao" or "Kung Po" means "palatial guardian," in reference to his official title. I love this spicy-sweet dish, but can't stand versions of it made with oyster sauce or cabbage. In my view, it should be numbingly spicy, sweet, and tangy. There are many variations of the dish and this is my home-style Western version. The tang comes from the Chinkiang black rice vinegar.

PREP TIME: 10 minutes • **COOK IN:** 10 minutes • **SERVES:** 2–4 to share

2 skinless chicken breasts or 4 thighs, cut into ½-inch slices

Salt and ground white pepper

1 tbsp of potato flour or cornstarch

1 tbsp of peanut oil

2 tbsps of Sichuan peppercorns

4 dried red chilies

1 tbsp of Shaohsing rice wine or dry sherry

1 red pepper, seeded and cut into chunks

2 scallions, chopped into 1-inch lengths

Handful of dry-roasted cashews

FOR THE SAUCE

7 tbsps of cold vegetable stock

1 tbsp of light soy sauce

1 tbsp of tomato ketchup

1 tbsp of Chinkiang black rice vinegar or balsamic vinegar

1 tbsp of hoisin sauce

1 tsp of chili sauce

1 tbsp of cornstarch

1. Place the chicken in a bowl and season with salt and pepper. Add the potato flour or cornstarch and mix well to coat the chicken pieces. Add all the ingredients for the sauce to another bowl and stir to combine.

2. Heat a wok over high heat until it starts to smoke and then add the peanut oil. Add the Sichuan peppercorns and dried chilies and fry for a few seconds, then add the chicken pieces and stir-fry for 2 minutes. As the chicken begins to turn opaque, add the rice wine or dry sherry. Cook for an additional 2 minutes, then pour in the sauce.

3. Bring to a boil, add the red pepper, and cook in the sauce with the chicken for another 2 minutes, or until the meat is cooked through and the sauce has thickened and become slightly sticky in consistency. Add the scallions and cook for 1 minute. Toss in the cashews, then transfer to a serving plate and serve immediately.

CHING'S TIP
For a darker sauce, you could add a small drop of dark soy sauce.

Sichuan chili tomato chicken

This dish brings together my two favorite ingredients. I love ripe heirloom tomatoes and I adore Sichuan peppercorns—their mouth-numbing spiciness is addictive.

PREP TIME: 10 minutes • **COOK IN:** 12 minutes • **SERVES:** 2–4 to share

1 tbsp of peanut oil

2 cloves of garlic, crushed

1 tbsp of peeled and roughly sliced fresh ginger

1 red chili, seeded and finely chopped

1 tbsp of Sichuan peppercorns

1 tbsp of chili bean paste

4 chicken thighs, boned and cut into 1½-inch pieces

1 tbsp of Shaohsing rice wine or dry sherry

2 large ripe heirloom tomatoes or beefsteak tomatoes, skin left on (see the tip below) and quartered

2 scallions, cut on the diagonal into 1-inch pieces

FOR THE SAUCE

1 tbsp of light soy sauce

⅔ cup cold vegetable stock

1. Heat a wok over high heat until it starts to smoke and then add the peanut oil. Add the garlic, ginger, chili, Sichuan peppercorns, and chili bean paste and stir well for just under a minute.

2. Add the chicken pieces and keep stirring until they start to turn opaque. Pour in the rice wine or dry sherry and cook for about 4 minutes, stirring continuously, then add the tomatoes and stir to combine.

3. Pour in the sauce ingredients, then bring to a boil and cook for 4 minutes, or until the chicken is cooked through. Add the scallions and cook for 1 minute, or until softened. Serve immediately with jasmine rice.

> **CHING'S TIP**
> There's no need to skin the tomatoes—the skin holds all the nutrients. If you want to skin them, however, see the tip on page 30.

Steamed chicken with Chinese mushrooms, goji berries, and dried lily bulbs

My grandmother used to prepare a similar dish to this on special occasions to which she would add dried Chinese dates and bamboo shoots. This is my re-creation of her recipe: the goji berries add sweetness and the lily bulbs give fragrance. Serve with jasmine rice.

PREP TIME: 10 minutes • **COOK IN:** 20 minutes • **SERVES:** 2

1 tbsp of peanut oil

2 tbsps of Shaohsing rice wine or dry sherry

1 tbsp of toasted sesame oil

2 chicken thighs, skinned and each piece halved on the bone (or use skinless, boneless chicken thighs)

1-inch piece of fresh ginger, peeled and sliced

2 dried Chinese mushrooms, soaked in hot water for 20 minutes, then drained and sliced, or 2 shiitake mushrooms, sliced

Salt and ground white pepper

1¼ oz dried lily bulbs, soaked in warm water for 20 minutes, then drained

Handful of dried goji berries, soaked in warm water for 20 minutes, then drained

1. Combine the peanut oil, rice wine or dry sherry, and toasted sesame oil in a bowl. Add the chicken, ginger, and sliced Chinese or shiitake mushrooms. Season with salt and pepper, then toss all the ingredients together and arrange on a small heatproof plate.

2. Lay the lily bulbs on top of the chicken and sprinkle with the goji berries, then place the plate inside a bamboo steamer. Set the steamer over a small pan of boiling water (making sure the bottom of the steamer doesn't touch the water) and steam over high heat for 20 minutes. Use a skewer to check that the chicken is cooked through, then remove from the heat and serve immediately.

Oyster-sauce chicken with ginger and shiitake mushrooms

This is one of my own flavor combinations, inspired by southern Chinese dishes from regions such as Canton and Fujian, where the combination of meat and seafood is very common. I hope you like it!

PREP TIME: 10 minutes • **COOK IN:** 9 minutes • **SERVES:** 2–4 to share

1 lb chicken thighs, skinned and the meatier parts sliced off but keeping some of the flesh on the bone (or use skinless, boneless chicken thighs)

Salt and ground white pepper

1 tbsp of potato flour or cornstarch

1 tbsp of peanut oil

1-inch piece of fresh ginger, peeled and sliced

1 tbsp of Shaohsing rice wine or dry sherry

5 shiitake mushrooms, sliced

2 large scallions, sliced on the diagonal

FOR THE SAUCE

1 tbsp of light soy sauce

1 tbsp of oyster sauce

1 tbsp of chili sauce

7 tbsps of cold vegetable stock

1. Place the chicken pieces in a bowl and season with salt and pepper. Add the potato flour or cornstarch and mix well to coat the chicken. Pour all the ingredients for the sauce into another bowl and stir together to combine.

2. Heat a wok over high heat until it starts to smoke and add the peanut oil. Add the ginger and fry for a few seconds, then add the chicken pieces and stir-fry for 4 minutes, stirring constantly.

3. As the chicken starts to turn opaque, add the rice wine or dry sherry and cook for an additional 2 minutes, then add the sauce and bring to a boil. Add the shiitake mushrooms and cook for 1 minute, then stir in the scallions. Remove from the heat and serve immediately.

Hoisin chicken

This recipe uses store-bought hoisin sauce to make a delicious marinade for coating the chicken before roasting it in the oven. The sweet flavor goes down well with children and makes it perfect as an accompaniment to other, saltier-tasting dishes. Great for a barbecue on a hot day, this is equally suitable for making at any time of year.

PREP TIME: 5 minutes, plus 20 minutes for marinating
COOK IN: 32 minutes • **SERVES:** 2–4 to share

1 lb chicken thighs and drumsticks, skin on
1 scallion, thinly sliced, to garnish

FOR THE MARINADE
1 tbsp of Shaohsing rice wine or dry sherry
2 tbsps of hoisin sauce
¼ cup light soy sauce
1 tbsp of dark soy sauce
1 tbsp of light brown sugar
1 tbsp of peanut oil
1-inch piece of fresh ginger, peeled and grated

1. Place all the marinade ingredients in a large bowl, then add the chicken pieces and toss in the marinade to coat. Cover the bowl with plastic wrap and place in the fridge to marinate for at least 20 minutes.

2. Meanwhile, preheat the oven to 350°F.

3. Remove the chicken pieces from the marinade (retaining the liquid) and place in a roasting pan. Roast in the oven for 30 minutes, or until cooked through and crisp on top.

4. Just before serving, pour the marinade into a small saucepan, bring to a boil, and drizzle over the chicken. Sprinkle over the scallion and serve with rice and salad or vegetables, such as the Bok Choy with Carrot and Garlic (see page 144).

Twice-cooked salt and pepper chicken

This is one of my favorite ways to cook a whole chicken. Organic is best, as there is less fat beneath the skin—the trick to getting a deliciously crisp skin. The chicken is first stuffed and boiled to infuse all the flavors, then roasted until the skin is golden.

PREP TIME: 20 minutes • COOK IN: 1 hour 40 minutes • SERVES: 4

One 4-lb 4-oz chicken

4-inch piece of fresh ginger, peeled and sliced

4 scallions, cut into 1-inch slices, white and green parts separated

5 dried Chinese mushrooms, soaked in hot water for 20 minutes, then drained and sliced, or 5 shiitake mushrooms, sliced

3 star anise

1 tbsp of Sichuan peppercorns

1 tsp of salt

¼ tsp of ground white pepper

2 tbsps of Shaohsing rice wine or dry sherry

11 oz jasmine rice

FOR THE SPICE RUB

1 tsp of sea salt

1 tsp of ground white pepper

1 tbsp of Chinese five-spice powder

1 tbsp of peanut oil

FOR THE DIPPING SAUCE

5 tbsps of olive oil

1 tbsp of ginger, finely chopped

1 tbsp of chili, finely chopped

1 tbsp scallion, finely chopped

1. Wash the chicken thoroughly and pat dry with paper towels, then stuff the cavity with the ginger, the white parts of the scallions, and the mushrooms.

2. Bring 10½ cups of water to a boil in a large saucepan or casserole. Put in the chicken with the star anise, Sichuan peppercorns, salt, pepper, and rice wine or dry sherry. Bring back to a boil, then reduce the heat to medium and simmer, uncovered, for 1 hour, removing any scum that rises to the surface.

3. Add the green parts of the scallions and cook for an additional 20 minutes, then remove the chicken and drain well, reserving the stock.

4. Preheat the oven to 425°F. Mix together the ingredients for the spice rub, then brush over the skin of the chicken. Place in a roasting pan and roast in the oven for 15 minutes, or until the skin is crisp and golden.

5. Meanwhile, rinse the rice and place in a saucepan. Pour in 2½ cups of the reserved chicken stock and bring to a boil. Reduce the heat to low, cover, and simmer for 20 minutes, or until the rice has absorbed the stock and is cooked and fluffy.

6. Remove the chicken from the oven and allow to rest. Carve and serve with the rice and dipping sauce.

Three-cup chicken

This Taiwanese recipe is so called because it uses 1 cup of soy sauce, 1 cup of toasted sesame oil, and 1 cup of rice wine. You can vary the amounts, but the final dish should be slightly sticky.

PREP TIME: 10 minutes • **COOK IN:** 14 minutes • **SERVES:** 2–4 to share

1 tbsp of peanut oil

5 cloves of garlic, finely chopped

1-inch piece of fresh ginger, peeled and sliced

4 chicken thighs, skin on, boned and cut into 1½-inch pieces

¼ cup light soy sauce

¼ cup toasted sesame oil

¼ cup Shaohsing rice wine or dry sherry

1 tbsp of light brown sugar

Small handful of Chinese basil leaves, or Thai or Italian sweet basil, plus extra to garnish

1 red chili, seeded and cut into strips, to garnish (optional)

1. Heat a wok over high heat until it starts to smoke and then add the peanut oil. Add the garlic and ginger and stir-fry for a few seconds, then add the chicken and stir-fry for 2–3 minutes, or until it has browned. Add the soy sauce, toasted sesame oil, and rice wine or dry sherry and cook over medium heat for 6 minutes. Stir well and add the sugar.

2. Bring to a boil, then reduce the heat and simmer for about 5 minutes, or until the sauce has reduced completely and the chicken is cooked through. Remove from the heat, stir in the basil leaves, and leave to wilt slightly.

3. Pour onto a serving plate, garnish with the chili strips if you like, and more basil leaves, and serve immediately with some jasmine rice.

> **CHING'S TIP**
> Since you want a dry stir-fry here, it's important to use toasted sesame oil, which will reduce as it cooks, and not pure sesame oil, which will just keep on cooking and not reduce.

Chili chicken and cashew nuts

The traditional technique for making this dish involves three or four stages. However, I have adapted the recipe so that the chicken is cooked in no time, giving you a tasty meal in minutes.

PREP TIME: 10 minutes • **COOK IN:** 7 minutes • **SERVES:** 2

3 chicken thighs, skinned, boned, and cut into ¾-inch chunks (or use skinless, boneless chicken thighs)

1 tsp of potato flour or cornstarch mixed with 1 tbsp of water

½ tsp of Chinese five-spice powder

2 tbsps of peanut oil

1 tsp of Sichuan peppercorns

1 tsp of chili bean paste

1 red chili, seeded and ground using a mortar and pestle

Dash of Shaohsing rice wine or dry sherry

3½ oz roasted salted cashews

2 scallions, sliced on the diagonal

1 tsp of light soy sauce, or to taste

½ lime

1. Place the chicken pieces in a bowl, add the potato flour or cornstarch paste, and turn to coat, then season with the five-spice powder.

2. Heat a wok over high heat until it starts to smoke and add the peanut oil. Add the Sichuan peppercorns, chili bean paste, and ground red chili and stir-fry for 30 seconds.

3. Add the chicken pieces and leave to settle in the wok for 30 seconds, then add the rice wine or dry sherry. Toss all the ingredients together and cook for 3–4 minutes, or until the chicken has turned virtually opaque.

4. Add the cashews and cook for another minute, then add the scallions, toss well, and cook for an additional minute. Season to taste with the soy sauce and add a squeeze of lime juice. Divide between plates and serve with egg-fried rice or plain rice.

Fruity sweet-and-sour duck

The Cantonese are known for their love of sweet-and-sour combinations, and this recipe comes from that region. It's a home-style dish—easy, fruity, and ready in minutes. I hope you enjoy it.

PREP TIME: 15 minutes • **COOK IN:** 5 minutes • **SERVES:** 2

Two 9-oz duck breasts, skinned and cut into thin slices

Sea salt and ground white pepper

1 tsp of Shaohsing rice wine or dry sherry

2 tbsps of potato flour or cornstarch

¾ cup peanut oil

1-inch piece of fresh ginger, peeled and thinly sliced

1 red pepper, seeded and cut into ½-inch chunks

2 oz peeled pineapple, cut into ½-inch cubes

Juice of 2 small oranges

Juice of 1 lime

1 tbsp of light soy sauce

Few orange segments, to garnish

1. Put the slices of duck breast into a bowl with some salt, white pepper, the rice wine or dry sherry, and the potato flour or cornstarch and mix well.

2. Place a wok over high heat and add the peanut oil. Heat the oil to 350°F, or until a cube of bread dropped in turns golden brown in 15 seconds and floats to the surface. Using a slotted spoon, add the duck and fry for about 2 minutes, or until crisp on the outside.

3. Take the wok off the heat, remove the duck from the hot oil, and drain on paper towels. Pour the oil from the wok through a sieve into a heatproof container and save to use later.

4. Set the wok back over high heat until it starts to smoke and then add 1 tbsp of the reserved peanut oil. Add the ginger and stir-fry for a few seconds, then add the red pepper and pineapple and stir-fry for an additional minute. Return the duck to the wok, season with the orange juice, lime juice, and soy sauce, and toss well.

5. Garnish with orange segments and serve immediately with Egg and Asparagus Fried Rice (see page 186).

Beef, Pork & Lamb

When I was growing up, meat was a luxury. We never ate lamb and beef was expensive and rare, so the meat most often served at our kitchen table was pork or chicken and sometimes duck (usually on a special occasion). Pork was and still is the meat most commonly eaten in a Chinese household. My father used to breed pigs for sale because it made money; he would never eat them and so grew up rarely eating pork. He would always say to us (and still does), "Do you know how lucky you are? All we had for breakfast was cold leftover rice with soy sauce!" Occasionally it would be cold roasted sweet potatoes instead, if he was lucky. He was one of eight children and mealtimes were a fight between him and his siblings. He was the lucky one, relatively speaking, because he was the eldest son and therefore the most treasured in the family, so he usually got more than the others.

Traditionally, pork was the most commonly consumed type of meat in China because dishes could be created using the whole animal. The pig's ears would be dried in the sun, then rehydrated and cooked in stir-fries. Its trotters would be stewed. The legs, shoulder, and tenderloin would be roasted, while the belly meat would be slow-cooked in a spiced soy stewing liquid and eaten with rice. Any leftover pork fat would be used to make dried pork sausages. The pig's heart and kidneys were used in broths or stir-fried, and the intestines stir-fried with ginger and rice wine or sometimes served with a chili sauce. Rice wine helped to kill any bacteria and mask any odors of meat that was past its best. My father said his favorite was the pig's tail, slow-cooked until the skin was so tender that it melted in the mouth.

It was only when I moved to South Africa from Taiwan that I began to eat, and enjoy, beef and lamb.

I remember on my first day at school being given a toasted ground beef sandwich with ketchup. It was the most delicious thing I had ever tasted, made all the more special by being given to me by Lindsay, my first school friend.

South Africans are well known for their love of *braais* (barbecues), and as I learned the way of life there, I attended many *braai* parties. I was introduced to different ways of eating and different cuts of meat like sirloin steak and racks of lamb. I also tried my first biltong (dried beef jerky), which became my favorite snack, as well as *boerewors* ("farmer's sausage"). Some were made with different herbs and seasonings; those made with pork fat were called *spekwors*. I also tried *droe-wors*, a type of dried sausage—much drier than, for example, salami. I also had gamey meat like ostrich and springbok. It was all so delicious—like being in meat heaven! This was such a different world from growing up in Taiwan, and if I thought I was in meat heaven, my father must have thought he was in paradise!

There is no shortage of meat on a takeout menu, of course. Takeout chefs know how to get the best out of the meat by using bones to make stock or tenderizing and marinating cheaper cuts to be used in delicious stir-fries. However, the beauty of creating your own takeout experience at home is that you can be more extravagant if you prefer. I have included some takeout classics but with a twist, such as Beef in Oyster Sauce with Choy Sum, Chili Peanut Beef, and Cantonese-Style Sweet-and-Sour Pork (see pages 100, 101, and 108). Most can be prepared within 30 minutes and are perfect for a midweek supper or for entertaining friends and family.

Beef in oyster sauce with choy sum

This makes a great instant supper for serving on a weekday—a classic takeout dish that's also perfect for cooking at home. Eat it carb-free or serve with rice.

PREP TIME: 10 minutes • **COOK IN:** 5 minutes • **SERVES:** 2

12 oz beef tenderloin

2 tbsps of peanut oil

FOR THE MARINADE

1 tsp of light soy sauce

1 tbsp of oyster sauce

Pinch of light brown sugar

Pinch of salt

Pinch of ground black pepper

FOR THE CHOY SUM

3 cloves of garlic, crushed and finely chopped

1 red chili, seeded and finely chopped

7 oz choy sum, sliced into 2½-inch lengths

Pinch of salt

1 tsp of oyster sauce

1. Prepare the beef tenderloin by tenderizing it with a meat mallet or the side of a Chinese cleaver. Slice it thinly and place the pieces in a bowl along with all the ingredients for the marinade. Stir in the marinade to coat and then set aside while you cook the choy sum.

2. Heat a wok over high heat until it starts to smoke and then add half the peanut oil. Add the garlic and chili and toss together quickly, then add the choy sum and mix in. Add a drop of water to help create some steam to cook the vegetables, then stir-fry for 1 minute. Season with the salt and the oyster sauce and transfer to a warmed serving plate.

3. Place the wok back over high heat and add the remaining peanut oil. Add the beef slices and stir-fry for 1–2 minutes. Place on top of the cooked choy sum and serve immediately.

Chili peanut beef

This dish is spicy and mouth-tinglingly delicious with a capital D. It's quick and easy to cook too!

PREP TIME: 5 minutes • **COOK IN:** 5 minutes • **SERVES:** 2–4 to share

9 oz beef tenderloin

1 tbsp of peanut oil

1 tbsp of Sichuan peppercorns

2 dried red chilies

1 tbsp of Shaohsing rice wine or dry sherry

Dash of chili oil

Dash of toasted sesame oil

Handful of dry-roasted peanuts

Small handful of cilantro, finely chopped (optional)

FOR THE SAUCE

1 tbsp of chili bean paste

1 tbsp of crunchy peanut butter

1 tbsp of light soy sauce

1 tbsp of Chinkiang black rice vinegar or balsamic vinegar

1 tbsp of cornstarch

1. Prepare the beef tenderloin by tenderizing it with a meat hammer or the side of a Chinese cleaver, then slice it into thin strips.

2. Heat a wok over high heat until it starts to smoke and then add the peanut oil. Add the Sichuan peppercorns and dried chilies and toss together for a few seconds, then add the slices of beef tenderloin and stir-fry for 30 seconds. As the meat starts to turn brown, add the rice wine or dry sherry.

3. Mix together the ingredients for the sauce and add to the wok, stirring well to combine with the beef, then bring to a boil.

4. Remove from the heat and drizzle over a little chili oil and toasted sesame oil. Add the peanuts and cilantro (if using) and toss together to combine, then transfer to a serving plate and serve immediately with rice and Special Mixed Vegetables (see page 155).

Beef with bean sprouts and scallions

If you want a tasty, effortless supper, you can't get any easier than this dish. A short time marinating, then speedy cooking in a hot wok ensures that dinner is on the table in no time. While the beef is marinating, you can boil some rice or, better still, make it in a rice cooker if you have one.

PREP TIME: 10 minutes, plus 20 minutes for marinating • **COOK IN:** 4 minutes • **SERVES:** 2

9 oz beef sirloin, fat removed and meat cut into ½-inch slices

1 tbsp of peanut oil

5 oz bean sprouts

1 tsp of cornstarch mixed with 1 tbsp of water

2 scallions, finely chopped

FOR THE MARINADE

2 cloves of garlic, crushed

2 tbsps of peeled and grated ginger

2 tbsps of light soy sauce

1 tsp of dark soy sauce

1 tsp of light brown sugar

2 tbsps of mirin

1. Place all the marinade ingredients in a large bowl, then add the beef slices and mix well to coat. Cover the bowl with plastic wrap and set the beef aside to marinate for 20 minutes.

2. Heat a wok over high heat until it starts to smoke and then add the peanut oil. Remove the beef from the bowl, reserving the marinade, and cook for 2 minutes.

3. Add the bean sprouts, reserved marinade, and the cornstarch paste, then toss together and cook for an additional minute. Stir in the finely chopped scallions, transfer to a serving plate, and serve immediately with jasmine rice.

Black pepper beef and rainbow vegetable stir-fry

My grandmother always said that if we ate vegetables of every color of the rainbow, we would stay as healthy as anything. This is the perfect way to ensure you get more than your five a day.

PREP TIME: 10 minutes, plus 20 minutes for marinating • **COOK IN:** 5 minutes • **SERVES:** 2–4

9 oz beef sirloin, fat removed and meat cut into ¼-inch slices

1 tbsp of cornstarch

2 tbsps of peanut oil

1-inch piece of fresh ginger, peeled and grated

11 oz mixture of sliced snow peas, broccoli, sugar snap peas, baby bok choy, red cabbage, ribbons of carrot, and baby scallions

Dash of light soy sauce or to taste

FOR THE MARINADE

1 tbsp of dark soy sauce

1 tbsp of light soy sauce

1 tbsp of Shaohsing rice wine or dry sherry

2 pinches of ground black pepper

1. Mix together the ingredients for the marinade in a large bowl, then add the beef and stir to coat. Cover the bowl with plastic wrap and set aside for 20 minutes to marinate, then remove from the marinade (reserving it) and dust with the cornstarch.

2. Heat a wok over high heat, and when it starts to smoke, add half the peanut oil. Add the ginger and stir-fry for a second or so, then add the vegetable mixture and toss together in the wok. Add a drop of water to create a little steam for cooking the vegetables. Cook for 1 minute and transfer to a plate.

3. Place the wok back over the heat and add the remaining peanut oil, followed by the beef. Let the meat settle for a few seconds, then stir in the wok for 1–2 minutes. Add the stir-fried vegetables and toss together with the beef. Season with additional light soy sauce, then transfer to a serving plate and eat immediately.

Xi'an-style beef curry in a hurry

Xi'an was the ancient capital of China and marked the end of the Silk Road, along which many spices found their way into the country. In the markets in central Xi'an, stalls still sell a huge array of spices, used to create a variety of spicy dishes, including curries.

Curry in one form or another is eaten throughout the country, so it is no surprise that it has a place on the Chinese takeout menu. Curry flavors will vary from place to place, but the spices almost always include turmeric, mild curry powder, dried chilies, and garam masala. This is my version of a Xi'an-style beef curry, with new potatoes, carrots, and peas to add sweetness and texture.

PREP TIME: 10 minutes • **COOK IN:** 10 minutes • **SERVES:** 2–4 to share

3 new potatoes (14 oz in total), peeled and cut into ½-inch chunks

1 carrot (3½ oz), cut into ½-inch chunks

11 oz beef sirloin, cut into ¾-inch chunks

1 tsp of turmeric

1 tsp of medium curry powder

Pinch of salt

Pinch of ground white pepper

1 tbsp of peanut oil

1 white onion, diced

1 star anise

1 tbsp of Shaohsing rice wine or dry sherry

3½ oz frozen peas

FOR THE SAUCE

1 tbsp of light soy sauce

1 tbsp of dark soy sauce

7 tbsps of cold chicken stock

2 tbsps of cornstarch

1. Place the potatoes and carrot in a saucepan of water, bring to a boil, and keep boiling for 5 minutes. Remove from the heat, drain, and refresh in cold water, then set aside.

2. Place the beef in a large bowl along with the turmeric, curry powder, and salt and pepper, and stir the meat in the spices to coat.

3. Heat a wok over high heat until it starts to smoke and then add the peanut oil. Add the onion and stir-fry until translucent, then add the star anise and the seasoned beef pieces. As the beef starts to turn brown at the edges, add the rice wine or dry sherry.

4. Pour in the ingredients for the sauce and bring to a boil, then add the parboiled potatoes and carrot, followed by the peas, and bring back up to a boil. Reduce the heat to medium and simmer for 2–3 minutes, then serve immediately with jasmine rice.

Cantonese-style sweet-and-sour pork

You will recognize this sweet-and-sour pork recipe as similar to that served in the Chinese restaurants in the US. However, some can be sickly sweet and the batter quite thick. This is my healthier and lighter version.

PREP TIME: 15 minutes • **COOK IN:** 12 minutes • **SERVES:** 2–4 to share

1 egg, beaten

1 tbsp of cornstarch

9 oz pork tenderloin, cut into ¼-inch slices

Salt and ground white pepper

1⅔ cups peanut oil

1-inch piece of fresh ginger, peeled and grated

1 red pepper, seeded and cut into chunks

1 green pepper, seeded and cut into chunks

One 8-oz can of pineapple chunks in juice, sliced

1 tbsp of light soy sauce

1 tbsp of clear rice vinegar or cider vinegar

½ tsp of light brown sugar (optional)

1 tsp of cornstarch mixed with 1 tbsp of water

1. Mix the egg and cornstarch together in a large bowl to make a batter. Stir the pork tenderloin slices in the mixture, seasoning with salt and pepper.

2. Place a wok over high heat and add the peanut oil. Heat the oil to 350°F, or until a cube of bread dropped in turns golden brown in 15 seconds and floats to the surface. Carefully lower the pork slices into the oil and fry for 3–4 minutes, or until golden brown. Lift out using tongs or a slotted spoon and place on a plate lined with paper towels to drain any excess oil.

3. Strain the oil into a heatproof container and save to use later. Retain 1 tbsp of the oil in the wok and heat until it starts to smoke. Add the grated ginger and the peppers and quickly stir in the wok to stop the ginger from sticking. Stir for 2 minutes, then add the sliced pineapple chunks and their juice from the can and bring to a boil.

4. Season with the soy sauce, vinegar, and brown sugar (if using), then as the liquid in the wok reduces and boils, thicken with the cornstarch paste. Tip the fried pork back into the wok, stirring and tossing together so that it is covered in the sauce. Remove from the heat and serve immediately with boiled rice and stir-fried vegetables.

Yin and yang crispy pork salad

The pork in this dish is marinated and fried, then served on a bed of fresh Boston lettuce leaves. Simple, delicious, well balanced, and full of flavor.

PREP TIME: 10 minutes, plus 20 minutes for marinating • **COOK IN:** 3 minutes • **SERVES:** 2

9 oz pork tenderloin, cut into ¼-inch slices

1⅔ cups peanut oil

2 oz potato flour or cornstarch

FOR THE MARINADE

1 tbsp of peeled and grated ginger

1 tbsp of Shaohsing rice wine or dry sherry

1 scallion, finely chopped

1 tsp of Sichuan peppercorns, toasted and ground (see the tip on page 49)

½ tsp of salt

1 tsp of light soy sauce

1 tsp of yellow bean sauce

1 tsp of hoisin sauce

Pinch of Chinese five-spice powder

TO SERVE

Boston lettuce leaves, sliced

1 tbsp of sesame seeds, toasted (see the tip on page 44)

1 scallion, thinly sliced

1. Mix the marinade ingredients together in a large bowl, add the pork, and stir to coat, then cover in plastic wrap, place in the fridge, and leave to marinate for a minimum of 20 minutes or preferably overnight.

2. Place a wok over high heat and add the peanut oil. Heat the oil to 350°F, or until a cube of bread dropped into the oil turns golden brown in 15 seconds and floats to the surface.

3. Dust the pork pieces in the potato flour or cornstarch and then place in the hot oil, frying for 2–3 minutes or until golden brown. Lift the pieces out using tongs or a slotted spoon and then drain on paper towels.

4. To serve, dress the serving plate with a bed of sliced Boston lettuce, then place the pork slices on top, sprinkle over the toasted sesame seeds, and scatter with the sliced scallion.

Black bean wok-fried ribs with bean sprouts and chilies

This tasty stir-fry uses chunky short ribs to allow for quick wok cooking. Fermented black beans and chilies add smoky and spicy flavors. It's perfect served with stir-fried vegetables and rice.

PREP TIME: 5 minutes • **COOK IN:** 10 minutes • **SERVES:** 2–4 to share

1 tbsp of peanut oil

2 cloves of garlic, crushed

1 red chili, seeded and finely chopped

1 tbsp of fermented salted black beans, rinsed and crushed

9 oz pork ribs, chopped into 1-inch pieces

1 tbsp of Shaohsing rice wine or dry sherry

Large handful of bean sprouts

1 tbsp of light soy sauce

1 tbsp of dark soy sauce

1 green chili, sliced

1. Heat a wok over high heat until it starts to smoke and then add the peanut oil. Add the garlic and red chili and stir quickly for a few seconds, then add the beans and stir for a few more seconds.

2. Add the pork ribs and stir-fry for 1 minute, then add the rice wine or dry sherry. Cook the ribs for 6 minutes or until browned, stirring continuously and adding a small dash of water to help cook the meat. Add the bean sprouts and both the light and dark soy sauce.

3. Stir in the sliced green chili and cook until the bean sprouts have wilted slightly but still retain a crunch. Remove from the heat and serve immediately.

Red-cooked bacon lardons, shiitake mushrooms, and chestnuts

Whenever winter draws in, I find myself craving stews and braised dishes. I love the "red-cooking" technique (referring to the color of the cooking liquid) and like to use it to create new dishes. For this recipe, I've used it for cooking bacon coupled with my favorite, earthy shiitake mushrooms and sweet, nutty roasted chestnuts. This is a dish that will keep your stomach warm and happy however cold it is outside.

PREP TIME: 5 minutes • **COOK IN:** 7 minutes • **SERVES:** 2–4 to share

1 tbsp of peanut oil

1 tbsp of Chinese five spice (whole spices)

3½ oz bacon, cut into lardons

1 tbsp of Shaohsing rice wine or dry sherry

1 tbsp of light soy sauce

1 tsp of dark soy sauce

1 tbsp of light brown sugar

4 shiitake mushrooms, sliced

10 peeled and pre-roasted chestnuts

2 scallions, sliced, to garnish

1. Heat a wok over high heat until it starts to smoke and then add the peanut oil. Add the whole spices and stir for a few seconds, then add the bacon lardons and cook for 1 minute or until fragrant and browned.

2. Pour in the rice wine or dry sherry and the light and dark soy sauce and add the sugar. Add the mushrooms and chestnuts and bring to a boil, stirring continuously.

3. When the liquid has reduced and the ingredients are slightly sticky with the red glaze, remove from the heat and garnish with the scallions. Serve immediately with some jasmine rice.

Fish-fragrant eggplant with pork

This is my take on a classic Sichuan eggplant dish (*yu xiang qiezi*) in which "fish-fragrant" is used to describe the savory smell of the stock. Traditionally the eggplant is "passed through the oil," i.e., fried, to give it a silken creamy texture. I've stir-fried it here, for a healthier option. I have also added ground pork and Sichuan peppercorns for a comforting winter dish that can be cooked in minutes.

PREP TIME: 10 minutes • **COOK IN:** 10 minutes • **SERVES:** 2–4 to share

2 tbsps of peanut oil

1 eggplant (about 7 oz), sliced into batons

2 cloves of garlic, crushed and finely chopped

1-inch piece of fresh ginger, peeled and grated

1 red chili, seeded and finely chopped

1 tbsp of Sichuan peppercorns

9 oz lean ground pork

1 tbsp of Shaohsing rice wine or dry sherry

2 scallions, cut on the diagonal into 1-inch slices

Salt and ground white pepper

FOR THE SAUCE

7 tbsps of vegetable stock

1 tbsp of light soy sauce

1 tbsp Chinkiang black rice vinegar or balsamic vinegar

1 tbsp of cornstarch

1. Heat a wok over high heat until it starts to smoke and then pour in half the peanut oil. Add the eggplant pieces and stir-fry for about 5 minutes or until browned, adding a dash of water now and then to soften the eggplant. Once it is cooked, transfer to a plate.

2. Reheat the wok and add the remaining peanut oil. Add the garlic, ginger, chili, and Sichuan peppercorns and stir-fry for a few seconds, then add the pork, breaking it up in the wok with a wooden spoon. As the pork starts to turn brown, add the rice wine or dry sherry and cook for 2 minutes.

3. Add the cooked eggplant to the pork, then pour in the sauce ingredients and bring to a boil. Reduce the heat, then add the scallions and cook for just under a minute or until softened. Season with salt and pepper and serve immediately with jasmine or brown rice.

Spicy lamb stew

This classic Chinese dish brings together spices from central China, chili bean paste from Sichuan, potatoes from the New World, and carrots from Europe—fusion cooking before the term was invented, you might say! Delicious and easy to make, it tastes even better if kept and eaten on the following day. Serve with *mantou* (Chinese-style steamed buns), pita bread, or buttered rolls.

PREP TIME: 10 minutes, plus 20 minutes for marinating
COOK IN: 1 hour • **SERVES:** 2–4 to share

14 oz lamb steak, cut into
½-inch cubes

7 oz new potatoes, peeled and
cut into ¾-inch chunks

3½ oz carrots, cut into ¾-inch
chunks

2 tbsps of peanut oil

2 shallots, diced

2 star anise

1 tbsp of Shaohsing rice wine
or dry sherry

1 tbsp of chili bean paste

2½ cups vegetable stock

1 tbsp of cornstarch mixed
with 1 tbsp of water

FOR THE SPICE PASTE
¼ tsp of hot chili powder

1 tsp of ground cumin

1 tsp of turmeric

1 tsp of medium curry powder

1 tsp of fennel seeds

1 tbsp of peanut oil

1. Mix together the ingredients for the spice paste in a large bowl, then add the lamb and stir to coat. Cover with plastic wrap and leave to marinate for 20 minutes.

2. Meanwhile, place the potatoes and carrots in a saucepan of water, bring to a boil, and keep boiling for 7 minutes. Remove from the heat, drain, and refresh under cold water, then set aside.

3. Heat a wok over high heat until it starts to smoke and then add the peanut oil. Add the shallots and star anise and stir-fry for 2 minutes. Add the marinated lamb chunks and stir-fry until they start to turn brown.

4. Add the rice wine or dry sherry and cook for 2 minutes, then add the chili bean paste and stir-fry for a few seconds. Pour in the stock and bring to a boil, then reduce the heat to medium and cook, uncovered, for 40 minutes. Add the parboiled potatoes and carrots and cook for another 5 minutes, then stir in the cornstarch paste to thicken the stew and serve immediately.

Fish & Shellfish

When we lived in Taiwan, a small gray-haired woman would ride by on her large bicycle with a bucket attached to the front. Wearing a tall pointed hat of woven bamboo and a large red handkerchief tied across her face, she would ring her bell whenever she passed my grandparents' home.

The dirty white bucket would be full of water with some small river fish or sometimes live farmed carp swimming around in it. Depending on what was in the bucket and what she had decided to cook that day, my grandmother would always buy something from the fish woman if she could.

When my parents came to visit us or when we had special guests, my grandmother would always cook fish. It was expensive and, after chicken or duck, the most prized form of meat. We hardly ever ate beef because cattle were bred for sale and oxen used for working the land.

My grandmother's favorite ways of preparing fish were either steamed or wok-fried with ginger and soy sauce. The fish was almost always served whole unless she had a craving for fish-head soup, in which case it would be chopped up and cooked in a broth with ginger, cilantro, and tofu.

There is a real etiquette to eating fish. Usually the best bits, including the head and belly, would be served to the elders first and then, as youngsters, we would be given the tail and leftovers. We were never allowed to turn the fish over: one side would be eaten and then the skeleton moved to one side before the lower fillet was touched. There is the Chinese superstition that if you turn the fish over, you will miss a journey or cause a boat to capsize! Whatever the case, nothing of the fish went to waste.

My grandmother would serve good-sized portions of fish for me and my brother, but he used to hate fish and would secretly put his portion inside my bowl when Grandmother wasn't looking. My grandmother used to tell us that if you ate fish, you would be as clever and quick as a fish, and I believed her so I always ate what I was given. Whenever my brother bullied me, I used to retaliate by telling him that I was cleverer than him because I ate fish and he didn't.

In Chinese culture, a fish is a symbol of wealth and fortune because the word for fish, *yu*, is also a homonym for wealth and abundance. At Chinese New Year, it is customary to use the phrase "*Nian nian you yu*" ("May you have great abundance every year"). That is why you see fish appearing on posters and decorations for Chinese New Year.

I didn't really appreciate the anatomy of a fish until I moved to South Africa. My uncle had come to stay with us and he was a fan of fishing. There were several lakes near where we lived where you could fish, and he used to take my brother and cousin. On one occasion, he and my brother came back looking really sheepish. My brother said they had been caught fishing at a nearby lake when they weren't allowed to and were approached by a warden. They had escaped a fine by pretending they didn't know a word of English, and judging by my uncle's manner, they must have gotten a really bad telling-off because he didn't go fishing for weeks after that.

It was my uncle who taught us how to clean a fish: he would do so expertly as soon as he had caught the fish and then pack it into a thermal bag. After killing the fish, he would scale the skin with his knife and then proceed to take out the gills, stomach, intestines, and heart. One time he gutted a fish in front of our dog, Guo Chung; he was barking so loudly we think he must have been traumatized by the experience, poor thing!

Despite the gore, Uncle would cook us all sorts of fishy dishes, whether grilled, steamed, or fried. Twenty years on, he is now a vegetarian! Who would have thought he would put his fishing days behind him. When I ask him about those times, he says he regrets killing so many fish, but he also says that my aunt made him stop because their business kept failing and she believed he was killing all their *yu*, or fortune. He still has a glint in his eye that tells me a part of him misses it. After all, there is nothing more pleasurable and natural than being at one with nature and catching and preparing your own food.

It is the fruits of the sea rather than the lake that appear on the takeout menu. Most takeout dishes use shrimp and sometimes scallops as the main ingredient, usually cooked in a sweet-and-sour, black bean, or spicy Sichuan sauce. I have included some of my favorite takeout flavors here but paired them in a different way, so you will find Black Bean Mussels, for instance, Jumbo Shrimp in Chili Tomato Sauce with Zucchini, or XO Sauce and Bok Choy Squid (see pages 122, 127, and 130). There are fish dishes too, such as Steamed Sea Bass in Spinach Sauce and Breaded Mackerel with Sichuan Pepper, Chili, and Salt (see pages 136 and 134)—a spicy Eastern twist on that classic British takeout, fish and chips.

Black bean mussels

Black beans are one of my all-time favorite ingredients. They're so versatile and work with all meats as well as seafood. This is a delicious dish, full of flavor and so quick. It's also great for dinner parties—just make sure you have a large enough wok!

PREP TIME: 15 minutes • **COOK IN:** 7 minutes • **SERVES:** 2–4 to share

1 lb mussels

1 tbsp of peanut oil

2 cloves of garlic, crushed and finely chopped

1-inch piece of fresh ginger, peeled and sliced

2 red chilies, seeded and finely chopped

1 tbsp of fermented salted black beans, rinsed and crushed

1 tbsp of Shaohsing rice wine or dry sherry

1 scallion, sliced on the diagonal into 1-inch pieces

FOR THE SAUCE

7 tbsps of vegetable stock

1 tbsp of light soy sauce

1 tbsp of dark soy sauce

1 tbsp of cornstarch mixed with 1 tbsp of water

1. First scrub the mussels, removing any bits of "beard" attached to the shells and discarding any that remain open when tapped against a hard surface.

2. Heat a wok over high heat until it starts to smoke and then add the peanut oil. Add the garlic, ginger, chilies, and black beans and stir-fry for a few seconds. Add the mussels and stir-fry for a few seconds more. As the shells start to open up, season with the rice wine or dry sherry.

3. Pour in the ingredients for the sauce, then bring to a boil and cook for 5 minutes, or until the sauce has reduced and thickened and all the shells have opened. (Discard any that remain unopened.) Stir in the scallion, then transfer to a large bowl and serve immediately.

Nutty shrimp, asparagus, and cashew stir-fry

The crunchy roasted cashews make this a very addictive dish. It is perfect served with some boiled rice and great as a midweek supper.

PREP TIME: 5 minutes • **COOK IN:** 7 minutes • **SERVES:** 2

7 oz tender asparagus spears, woody ends snapped off, then cut into thirds

1 tbsp of peanut oil

2 cloves of garlic, crushed and finely chopped

1-inch piece of fresh ginger, peeled and grated

5 oz cooked shelled and deveined tiger shrimp

1 tbsp of Shaohsing rice wine or dry sherry

1 tbsp of light soy sauce

1 tsp of clear rice vinegar or cider vinegar

Handful of roasted salted cashews

1 tsp of cornstarch mixed with 1 tbsp of water

1 tbsp of toasted sesame oil

1. Bring a small saucepan of water to a boil, add the asparagus pieces, and blanch for 2 minutes, then drain and refresh under cold running water to stop them from cooking further. Put on a plate and set aside.

2. Heat a wok over high heat until it starts to smoke and then add the peanut oil. Add the garlic and ginger and stir-fry a few seconds, then add the blanched asparagus pieces. Stir-fry for 2 minutes and then add the shrimp and stir-fry for another minute.

3. Add the rice wine or dry sherry, followed by the soy sauce, vinegar, and cashews. Add the cornstarch paste to thicken the sauce, stir in the toasted sesame oil, and serve immediately.

Spicy sweet jumbo shrimp

This is a take on my mum's ketchup shrimp, which are really delicious. I have simply added chili to give it a kick. Sweet, spicy, and tangy, this dish is delicious with boiled rice and some steamed vegetables.

PREP TIME: 10 minutes • **COOK IN:** 5 minutes • **SERVES:** 2–4 to share

1 tbsp of peanut oil

1-inch piece of fresh
    ginger, peeled and sliced

11 oz raw jumbo shrimp in the
    shell, deveined (see the tip
    below)

1 tbsp of Shaohsing rice wine
    or dry sherry

2 tbsps of tomato ketchup

2 tbsps of chili sauce

1 scallion, sliced,
    to garnish

1. Heat a wok over high heat until it starts to smoke and then add the peanut oil. Add the ginger and fry for 1 second, then immediately add the shrimp and stir-fry for 1 minute.

2. As the shrimp start to turn pink, add the rice wine or dry sherry and cook for 2 minutes, then season with the ketchup and chili sauce. Toss well in the wok, then garnish with the sliced scallion and serve immediately.

> **CHING'S TIP**
> To devein the shrimp, simply run a sharp knife along the back of each shrimp and remove the vein with the tip of the knife. My grandmother would use a toothpick—pierce the skin between the head and body and pull the toothpick along the length, pulling the vein out with it. This ensures that the flesh and shell stay intact; cooking the shrimp with the shell on seals in the flavor and juices.

Healthy sweet-and-sour jumbo shrimp stir-fry

This is such a simple sweet-and-sour dish, made with delicious jumbo shrimp and a quick and easy sauce—a stir-fry that's ready in minutes.

PREP TIME: 10 minutes • **COOK IN:** 7 minutes • **SERVES:** 2

2 oz canned pineapple chunks

¾ cup pineapple juice

2 tbsps of peanut oil

6 large raw shelled and deveined jumbo shrimp, tails left on

1 tbsp of peeled and grated fresh ginger

1 red chili, seeded and finely chopped

½ onion, cut into chunks

Small handful of red and yellow pepper chunks

Small handful of bean sprouts

Salt and ground white pepper

Juice of 1 small lime

1 tsp of honey

1 scallion, thinly sliced, to garnish

1. Place the pineapple chunks and juice in a blender and whiz to a puree, then remove from the blender and set aside.

2. Heat a wok over high heat until it starts to smoke and then add half the peanut oil. Add the shrimp and stir-fry for 2–3 minutes or until they turn pink, then set aside.

3. Heat the remaining peanut oil in the wok and stir-fry the ginger and chili for a few seconds, then add the onion and stir-fry for 1 minute or until softened.

4. Add the pineapple puree and let the sauce reduce for 1 minute, then stir in the pepper chunks and bean sprouts and cook for another minute.

5. Season to taste with salt and pepper and add the lime juice and honey, then add the cooked shrimp and stir together. Check the seasoning, adding more if necessary, and sprinkle with the scallion. Serve immediately with boiled jasmine rice.

Jumbo shrimp in chili tomato sauce with zucchini

First you make the chili tomato paste and then add jumbo shrimp for a tasty, addictive dish. If you fancy a change from boiled rice, add some cooked egg noodles at the end to turn this into a spicy chow mein.

PREP TIME: 10 minutes • **COOK IN:** 5 minutes • **SERVES:** 2

1 tbsp of peanut oil

1 red chili, seeded and finely chopped

1 zucchini, grated

12 oz large raw shelled and deveined jumbo shrimp

1 tbsp of Shaohsing rice wine or dry sherry

1 tbsp of light soy sauce or to taste

Small handful of chopped cilantro

FOR THE TOMATO PASTE

1 onion, diced

1 red chili, seeded and roughly chopped

2 small ripe tomatoes, roughly chopped

2 tbsps of tomato ketchup

1 tbsp of light brown sugar

1 tbsp of light soy sauce

1. Put all the ingredients for the tomato paste into a blender and whiz together. Remove from the blender and set aside.

2. Heat a wok over high heat until it starts to smoke and then add the peanut oil. Add the red chili and fry for a few seconds, then add the zucchini and stir-fry for 1 minute.

3. Add the shrimp and cook for 30 seconds, adding the rice wine or dry sherry as the shrimp start to turn pink. Add the tomato paste, then bring to a boil and cook for 2 minutes.

4. Season to taste with the soy sauce, then garnish with the chopped cilantro and serve immediately.

Steamed jumbo shrimp with yellow bean sauce and garlic spinach

This dish is perfect for an intimate meal for two. Delicious as well as healthy, it's not exactly takeout fare, but an adapted version of this recipe—such as stir-fried shrimp in yellow bean sauce—would certainly work well as a takeout dish!

PREP TIME: 10 minutes • **COOK IN:** 10 minutes • **SERVES:** 2

2 giant jumbo shrimp in the shells, deveined (see the tip on page 124)

1-inch piece of fresh ginger, peeled and sliced into matchsticks

1 tbsp of Shaohsing rice wine or dry sherry

1 red chili, seeded and finely chopped, or 1 scallion, finely chopped, to garnish (optional)

FOR THE SAUCE

1 tbsp of peanut oil

2 cloves of garlic, crushed

2 tbsps of yellow bean sauce

¼ cup vegetable stock

1 tsp of light soy sauce

FOR THE GARLIC SPINACH

1 tbsp of peanut oil

1 clove of garlic, crushed and finely chopped

2 large handfuls of baby spinach leaves

1 pinch of sea salt

1. Place the shrimp on a heatproof plate that will fit inside a large bamboo steamer. Scatter the ginger on top and drizzle with the rice wine or dry sherry. Place the steamer over a wok or saucepan filled with boiling water (making sure the bottom of the steamer does not touch the water). Put the lid on and steam the shrimp over high heat for 8 minutes.

2. Meanwhile, for the sauce, heat a small wok over high heat until it starts to smoke and then add the peanut oil. Add the garlic and stir for a few seconds, then add the yellow bean sauce, stock, and soy sauce, and stir to combine. Bring to a boil, then reduce the heat to very low to keep warm.

3. Heat another small wok or saucepan over medium heat and add the peanut oil. Add the garlic and stir for a few seconds, then add the spinach and toss in the garlic oil until wilted. Season with the salt and set aside.

4. To serve, remove the shrimp from the steamer and place one on each plate. Keeping the head and tail on, peel away just one side of the shell of each shrimp to expose the meat, then drizzle over 2 tbsps of the sauce. Decorate with the garlic from the sauce. Spoon a mound of spinach on the plate, garnish with the chopped red chili or scallion, and serve immediately.

XO sauce and bok choy squid

XO sauce is the crème de la crème of Cantonese sauces. It is made from chopped dried seafood, such as shrimp and scallops, and dried fish, cooked with garlic, onions, and chili, and preserved in oil. The name XO comes from "Extra-Old," referring to extra-old Cognac, a symbol of luxury and quality; hence the term "XO" indicates something that is the ultimate in quality.

PREP TIME: 10 minutes • **COOK IN:** 5 minutes • **SERVES:** 2–4 to share

1 tbsp of peanut oil

1 tbsp of peeled and grated fresh ginger

2 dried red chilies

2 large bok choy, cut into strips

1 lb squid, cleaned, chopped into 2-inch pieces, and scored criss-cross fashion on the underside of the skin

1 tbsp of Shaohsing rice wine or dry sherry

2 tbsps of XO sauce

1 tbsp of light soy sauce

1. Heat a wok over high heat until it starts to smoke and then add the peanut oil. Add the ginger and chilies and fry for 1 second. Add the bok choy and stir-fry for another few seconds, then add the squid and stir-fry for 2 minutes.

2. As the squid starts to turn opaque and curl up, add the rice wine or dry sherry. Pour in the XO sauce and stir all the ingredients together. Season with the soy sauce and serve immediately with jasmine or brown rice.

Ginger and mushroom wined clams

This dish is warming, light, and earthy in flavor. You could always turn it into a nourishing broth by adding more vegetable stock and have it with some slices of buttered soda bread for a light supper, which would give you the best of East and West.

PREP TIME: 15 minutes • **COOK IN:** 7 minutes • **SERVES:** 2

11 oz clams

1 tbsp of peanut oil

1-inch piece of fresh ginger, peeled and sliced into matchsticks

2 tbsps of dried shrimp, soaked in hot water for 20 minutes, then drained (optional)

3 dried Chinese mushrooms, soaked in hot water for 20 minutes, then drained and sliced, or 3 shiitake mushrooms, sliced

¼ cup Shaohsing rice wine or dry sherry

7 tbsps of vegetable stock

Salt and ground white pepper

1 tbsp of cornstarch mixed with 1 tbsp of water

Large handful of cilantro

1. First scrub the clams, removing any debris from the shells and discarding any that remain open when tapped against a hard surface.

2. Heat a wok over high heat until it starts to smoke and then add the peanut oil. Add the ginger, dried shrimp (if using), and mushrooms and stir-fry for a few seconds. Add the clams and stir-fry for 1 minute.

3. As the shells start to open up, add the rice wine or dry sherry. Pour in the stock and cook for 3–4 minutes, or until all the shells have opened. Discard any that remain closed.

4. Season to taste with salt and pepper and thicken the cooking liquid with the cornstarch paste. Toss in the cilantro and let it wilt slightly, then remove from the heat, transfer to a large dish, and serve immediately.

Breaded mackerel with Sichuan pepper, chili, and salt

This is my way of incorporating oily fish into my diet. Of course you can also wok-fry mackerel with garlic, ginger, light soy sauce, toasted sesame oil, rice wine, and a pinch of sugar, and serve with boiled rice and steamed vegetables, but I also love this naughty "yang" way of cooking it.

PREP TIME: 10 minutes • **COOK IN:** 10 minutes • **SERVES:** 2

11 oz mackerel fillets, skin on
¼ cup all-purpose flour
2 eggs, beaten
⅔ cup panko breadcrumbs
1 tbsp of Sichuan peppercorns, toasted and ground (see the tip on page 49)
1 tbsp of dried chili flakes
½ tsp of sea salt
2 cups peanut oil

1. Rinse the mackerel fillets in cold running water and pat dry on paper towels. Cut the fillets into 1½-inch slices and set aside. Place the flour, beaten eggs, and breadcrumbs in three separate bowls.

2. In another small bowl, mix the ground Sichuan peppercorns with the chili flakes and sea salt and set aside.

3. Place a wok over high heat, then pour in the peanut oil and heat to 350°F, or until a cube of bread dropped in turns golden brown in 15 seconds and floats to the surface.

4. Place a piece of the fish in the flour (shaking off any excess flour), then dip into the egg and coat in the breadcrumbs. Repeat with all the pieces of fish and place in a bowl, then carefully lower one batch into the hot oil using a slotted spoon. When the batter turns golden brown, lift out the fish and drain any excess oil on a plate lined with paper towels and keep warm. Continue until all the fish has been cooked.

5. Sprinkle the spice mixture over the fish, toss together well, and serve immediately with thick-cut fries or, for a healthier alternative, shredded lettuce leaves, thin carrot strips, and sliced fresh chilies.

Steamed sea bass with ginger and mushrooms

In China, fish are mostly cooked whole, including the head, because the cheek (just below the eyes) is considered the best part. The eyes and lips are a delicacy too. Keeping the fish whole during cooking also symbolizes completeness and unity, which is important for Chinese New Year and other auspicious events in the Chinese calendar. The relatively large amount of rice wine provides a fragrant bittersweet flavor and works wonderfully well with the aromatic mushrooms, hot ginger, tangy scallions, and of course the sweet flesh of the fish.

PREP TIME: 10 minutes • **COOK IN:** 11 minutes • **SERVES:** 2–4 to share

1 whole sea bass (about 14 oz), gutted and scaled

Salt and ground white pepper

2-inch piece of fresh ginger, peeled and sliced

4 dried Chinese mushrooms, soaked in hot water for 20 minutes, then drained, stems removed, and sliced, or 4 shiitake mushrooms, sliced

¼ cup Shaohsing rice wine or dry sherry

2 oz oyster mushrooms

2 scallions, sliced lengthwise into 3-inch lengths

1. Place the fish on a heatproof plate that will fit inside a bamboo steamer. Cut a few slits in the skin on both sides, then season with salt and pepper. Place some slices of ginger and Chinese or shiitake mushroom into the slits and inside the fish.

2. Sprinkle over the rice wine or dry sherry, then place the plate in the steamer and close the lid. Set the steamer over a wok or saucepan filled with boiling water (making sure the bottom of the steamer doesn't touch the water) and steam over high heat for 8–9 minutes, or until the fish is cooked and the flesh flakes easily to the point of a knife.

3. Lay the oyster mushrooms and scallions on top of the fish and steam for an additional 2 minutes. Remove the steamer from the wok or pan, keeping the lid closed until ready to serve. Serve with jasmine rice and stir-fried vegetables.

> **ALSO TRY**
> You may use any white-fleshed fish for this dish and you could steam fillets rather than the whole fish, if you prefer.

Steamed sea bass in spinach sauce

This is a delicious way to serve steamed sea bass—in a spinach and garlic sauce. It's easy to make, nutritious, and fuss-free. The hardest part is getting your hands on the freshest-possible fish.

PREP TIME: 10 minutes • **COOK IN:** 10 minutes • **SERVES:** 2

2 wild sea bass fillets

Sea salt and ground white pepper

1 tbsp of Shaohsing rice wine or dry sherry

1 tbsp of peeled and grated fresh ginger

1 tbsp of light soy sauce or to taste

1 tbsp of cornstarch mixed with 1 tbsp of water

FOR THE SAUCE

1 tbsp of peanut oil

3 cloves of garlic, crushed

1 red chili, seeded and finely chopped

Large bunch of cilantro

Large handful of spinach leaves

7 tbsps of cold vegetable stock

1. Place the sea bass fillets on a heatproof plate that will fit inside a bamboo steamer. Season the fish with salt and pepper, drizzle over the rice wine or dry sherry, and rub the grated ginger over the flesh of the fish.

2. Put the plate inside the steamer and cover with the lid. Set the steamer over a wok or saucepan filled with boiling water (making sure the bottom of the steamer does not touch the water). Steam for 10 minutes over high heat, or until the flesh of the fish flakes easily to the point of a knife. Keep the fish warm in the steamer until ready to serve.

3. Meanwhile, place all the ingredients for the sauce in a blender and blitz together, then set aside.

4. Heat a small wok or saucepan over high heat and pour in the sauce, then season to taste with the soy sauce. Bring the sauce to a simmer, add the cornstarch paste and stir until thickened, then remove from the heat. Transfer the sea bass fillets to individual plates, pour over the sauce, and serve with Special Mixed Vegetables (see page 155) and jasmine rice.

> **ALSO TRY**
> This recipe can be adapted for any white-fleshed fish, including pollack or haddock.

Steamed flounder with black beans

Black bean sauce is a popular ingredient in so many takeout dishes. There is no need to buy it, however, because you can just as easily use the whole beans, and they taste so much better. I love pairing the beans with fish, as in this recipe inspired by a Cantonese dish served in Chinese restaurants. I've simply substituted flounder for the sea bass or pomfret that is usually incorporated in this dish.

PREP TIME: 5 minutes • **COOK IN:** 10 minutes • **SERVES:** 2 to share

1 whole flounder (about 1 lb 5 oz), gutted and scaled

1-inch piece of fresh ginger, peeled and sliced into matchsticks

1 tbsp of Shaohsing rice wine or dry sherry

1 tbsp of light soy sauce

1 tbsp of fermented salted black beans, rinsed and lightly crushed

2 scallions, sliced lengthwise

1. Score the sides of the flounder, then stuff the ginger slices into the slits as well as the body of the fish.

2. Place the fish on a heatproof plate that will fit inside a large bamboo steamer and drizzle the rice wine or dry sherry over the fish, followed by the soy sauce. Sprinkle over the black beans, then drape the scallions over the fish and place the lid on the steamer.

3. Place the steamer over a wok or saucepan filled with boiling water (making sure the bottom of the steamer does not touch the water) and steam the flounder over high heat for 10 minutes, or until the flesh of the fish has turned opaque and flakes easily when poked with a chopstick or knife.

4. Remove from the steamer and serve with Buddha's Stir-Fried Mixed Vegetables or Bok Choy with Carrot and Garlic (see pages 156 and 144) and some boiled rice.

Vegetarian

When I was 13, I turned vegetarian for almost a year, inspired by a trip to Taiwan. It was the summer holidays and my brother and I had gone back to visit my mum. She and my father had decided to set up an import–export business. She would be based in Taipei and my father would stay in London to look after us. It wasn't ideal, but my parents wanted my brother and me to have the best education possible and it seemed the only way forward after several failed business attempts following our move to London in 1989 and recession hitting in 1990.

We were happy to see Mum and spent some time with her in Taipei as well as visiting my grandparents and all the relatives in Kaohsiung, in the south. After visiting our relatives, my mum suggested we go to the Tzu-Chi Foundation based in the small village of Hua Lien, on the eastern coast of Taiwan. The Tzu-Chi abode is a special place, set up by a Buddhist nun, the venerable Master Cheng-Yen, an incredible woman with a big heart. Thousands of volunteers sign up each year to give their time to help with the organization's many charitable causes.

The abode is a beautiful, serene place. Two nuns with beaming, welcoming smiles greeted us. They led us to a courtyard with a temple behind it and we bowed to show our respect. The whole place was very quiet, so quiet you could hear the birds chirping. One of the nuns led us to a small building where there was a strong smell of incense. She said the Master Cheng-Yen would be able to see us in a few minutes. We sat on small round wooden stools and sipped oolong tea. We were all very excited and waited with nervous anticipation. Master Cheng-Yen came into the room and was introduced by another nun. She was a small fragile woman with bright eyes and a warm smile. I don't know what happened but I was overcome with emotion and the tears flowed naturally; I was unable to stop them. The master patted me on the head and told me to stop crying. She asked me whether I could write Chinese. I replied that I wasn't very good at it and she told me to try harder and never to forget where I was from. My mum's friend, who was accompanying us, said that she also cried the first time she saw the master and she told me it was a sign of "coming home."

At 12 noon a bell rang to signal that it was time for lunch. We were shown to the main dining room where we sat down on stools at simple round wooden tables. The dishes were already laid out, with the smell of rice wafting through the air. There must have been over a hundred people in that dining room, but there wasn't a sound. We said a blessing and then we had to take a grain of rice first from the eastern part of the bowl, then the western part and then the middle, to show our appreciation of the dish. Then we helped ourselves to an array of delicacies, all of which were vegetarian. There were stir-fried vegetables, braised bean curd, and stir-fried wheat gluten and tofu—all simply cooked but full of flavor. When the meal was over, we poured a small amount of hot water into our bowls and, using a piece of vegetable, "washed" the dish and then drank the liquid—a ritual called *xi-fu* ("preserving fortune"), acknowledging what a blessing it is to have food and that none should be wasted, for wasted food is a sign of wasted fortune. At the end of the meal, not one bowl had a speck of food left in it. It was a life-changing experience.

The nuns grew their own vegetables, made candles, and sewed socks, which they sold to make a living. The master's wise Buddhist teachings and quotes were published in books and sold to raise money to support the place. The whole community was self-sufficient and any profits were donated to charity. That afternoon, I helped the nuns pick vegetables and wash and prepare them for dinner, listened to their stories, and learned more about Buddhism. I was so moved by the whole experience that when we left I told my mum I was going to be a vegetarian, and I was for almost a year.

Sad to say that the dish that broke me was the hot bacon sandwiches served at breaktime at school! But I have never forgotten what I learned at Tzu-Chi: following the Buddhists' etiquette at the table, inspired by their compassion for all living beings, I always say a blessing of thanks for the animals that have sacrificed their lives.

Good Buddhists themselves, my grandparents always treasured the animals they kept on their farm. They ate chicken only if it was too old to lay eggs, while pigs were bred to sell and eaten only on special occasions. On the 15th of the lunar calendar every month, we ate only vegetables, to show our compassion for animals. I still try to do this every month, and I have my family to thank for making me a more mindful and considerate cook.

Vegetarian dishes are usually quite limited on a standard takeout menu. If I were running my own takeout shop or diner, I'd serve far more, and I've tried to expand the range here, offering a variety of recipes that would work either as side dishes or as a meal in their own right.

Bean sprout and scallion stir-fry

This is a simple, tasty, and economical dish that is very quick to make. To a Chinese cook, bean sprouts are the equivalent of potatoes to a Western cook. The most commonly used vegetable in Chinese cuisine, they add texture and crunch to a huge range of dishes, from stir-fries and soups to salads.

PREP TIME: 5 minutes • **COOK IN:** 3 minutes • **SERVES:** 2–4 to share

1 tbsp of peanut oil
1-inch piece of fresh
   ginger, peeled and sliced
Handful of bean sprouts
1 tbsp of light soy sauce
1 scallion, thinly sliced

Heat a wok over high heat until it starts to smoke. Add the peanut oil and ginger and fry for a few seconds. Add the bean sprouts and toss, then add a small dash of water to create some steam and cook for 1 minute, or until the bean sprouts start to wilt. Season with the soy sauce, stir in the scallion, and serve immediately.

Bok choy with carrot and garlic

Bok choy is a leafy vegetable much used in Chinese cooking, especially soups and stir-fries. I love both the green- and white-stemmed varieties.

PREP TIME: 5 minutes • **COOK IN:** 4 minutes • **SERVES:** 2–4 to share

1 tbsp of peanut oil
1 clove of garlic, crushed and
   finely chopped
1 small carrot, thinly sliced on
   the diagonal
7 oz baby bok choy, leaves
   separated (see the
   tip below)
2 pinches of coarse sea salt

Heat a wok over high heat until it starts to smoke, then add the peanut oil and the garlic and cook for a few seconds. Add the carrot slices and stir-fry for 2 minutes. Add the bok choy leaves and toss. Add a small dash of water and cook for 1 minute. Sprinkle over the sea salt and serve immediately.

CHING'S TIP
If you are using the larger, green-stemmed bok choy, then separate the leaves from the stalks, slice the stalks, and stir-fry with the carrot for 2 minutes before adding the leaves and stir-frying for 1 additional minute.

Lotus root salad

Lotus flowers have been grown in China for thousands of years. Several parts of the plant are edible, including the stem, also known as the root, which can be bought from Chinese supermarkets, sold fresh in vacuum packs. The roots are knobbly in appearance, and when you slice through one crosswise, you can see a series of holes, rather like the "rose" of a watering can. Look out for firm short roots without any markings. You can eat lotus roots raw, although I prefer to blanch mine in boiling water for a few minutes to get rid of any unwanted bacteria, since these grow buried in muddy waters. Delightfully crunchy and sweet, they resemble water chestnuts in texture, with a delicate flavor like bamboo shoots.

PREP TIME: 10 minutes, plus 20 minutes for chilling
COOK IN: 2 minutes • **SERVES:** 2–4 to share

7 oz fresh lotus roots

Small handful of cilantro, finely chopped, to garnish

1 red chili, seeded and finely chopped (optional)

FOR THE DRESSING

1 tbsp of toasted sesame oil

1 tbsp of clear rice vinegar or cider vinegar

1 tbsp of light soy sauce

Pinch of salt

Pinch of superfine sugar

1. To prepare the lotus roots, first cut through the joints between the segments, then peel the skin and place in a saucepan of boiling water to blanch for 2 minutes. Rinse in cold water to refresh, then slice thinly, using a mandoline if possible.

2. Mix together the ingredients for the dressing in a large bowl, then add the sliced lotus roots and toss in the dressing to coat. Cover with plastic wrap and chill for 20 minutes in the fridge. Serve garnished with the chopped cilantro and fresh chili.

Sweet roasted vegetables

Sweet potatoes are thought to have originated in tropical South America and then made their way to Europe. Chinese explorers are believed to have brought these to Asia in the mid-fifteenth century. They were certainly common enough when we were growing up in Taiwan. We used to wrap them in newspaper and "kong" them—that is, bury them in a hole in the ground filled with hot charcoal and allow them to slow-cook for a few hours until tender. It was the most delicious thing! I also love them roasted Western-style with other sweet vegetables and Chinese spices. It makes a great accompaniment to a Chinese roast.

PREP TIME: 20 minutes • **COOK IN:** 20 minutes • **SERVES:** 2–4 to share

2 red peppers, seeded and chopped into 2-inch pieces

2 red onions, cut into wedges

2 sweet potatoes (unpeeled), sliced into wedges

2 parsnips (unpeeled), sliced into wedges

¼ cup peanut oil or olive oil

2 tsps of honey

FOR THE SPICE MIX

1 tsp of sea salt

1 tsp of black peppercorns

1 tbsp of light brown sugar

1 tbsp of Chinese five-spice powder

1 small piece of cassia bark or cinnamon stick

2 cloves

1 star anise

1. Preheat the oven to 350°F.

2. Put all the spices in a spice grinder, or use a mortar and pestle and grind them into a fine powder.

3. Place all the prepared vegetables in a roasting pan and toss together. Sprinkle the spice mix over the vegetables and drizzle over the peanut oil or olive oil and the honey. Toss together in the pan and then roast in the oven for 20 minutes, or until golden.

Yellow bean sesame spinach

This makes a simple but elegant accompaniment to any meat or fish dish, or served with stir-fried vegetables for a vegetarian option. It is very quick to make and full of flavor. If you can, try to buy leafier savoy or semi-savoy spinach, with larger leaves, as opposed to baby spinach.

PREP TIME: 10 minutes • **COOK IN:** 5 minutes • **SERVES:** 2–4 to share

1 lb fresh young spinach

4 tsps of white sesame seeds, toasted (see the tip on page 44)

FOR THE SAUCE

1 tbsp of peanut oil

1 tsp of peeled and grated fresh ginger

1 tsp of yellow bean sauce

1 tbsp of light soy sauce

¼ cup cold vegetable stock

1 tsp of cornstarch mixed with 1 tbsp water

1. Bring a large saucepan of water to a boil. Add the spinach leaves and blanch for 20 seconds, then remove and drain well in a colander. Rinse the wilted leaves under cold running water, then squeeze out the excess water and set aside.

2. Heat a wok over high heat until it starts to smoke, then add all the ingredients for the sauce and bring to a boil. Allow the sauce to thicken and then remove from the heat.

3. Form the drained spinach into a log shape, about 4 inches long, then slice it into quarters. Stand the log shapes on a serving plate, top with the toasted sesame seeds, and drizzle the sauce around the plate using a spoon. Serve immediately.

Dou miao with enoki mushrooms

Dou miao are the immature shoots of the sugar snap pea or snow pea and are prized for their super-tender, sweet, and delicious stems. They can be found in Chinese supermarkets, although they are more expensive than other leafy greens used in Chinese cuisine. Usually they are added to soups at the last minute, or cooked in a simple stir-fry with stock and some garlic and ginger. I love to serve them stir-fried with enoki mushrooms. These have a very long, thin stem with a tiny golden head (hence their other name, golden needle mushrooms) and in the wild can be found growing on the Chinese hackberry tree. They can be eaten raw or added to stir-fries at the end of cooking to retain their sweet and delicate flavor. This is an elegant recipe, great as an accompaniment for the main dish at a dinner party.

PREP TIME: 5 minutes • **COOK IN:** 3 minutes • **SERVES:** 2–4 to share

1 tbsp of peanut oil
Few pinches of coarse sea salt
2 cloves of garlic, crushed and finely chopped
7 oz *dou miao* shoots
3½ oz enoki mushrooms
7 tbsps of vegetable stock
Pinch of ground white pepper

1. Heat a wok over high heat until it starts to smoke and then add the peanut oil. Add the sea salt followed by the garlic and then add the *dou miao* and stir-fry together for 2 minutes, or until the leaves wilt.

2. Break in the enoki mushrooms and toss all the ingredients together. Pour in the vegetable stock, season with the ground white pepper, and serve immediately.

Oriental mushrooms with black bean sauce

In this dish, the mushrooms act like a sponge to soak up all the delicious flavors of the black bean sauce. You can buy prepared black bean sauce, but there is nothing more rewarding than making your own: it's easy and quick, and packs a far more powerful flavor!

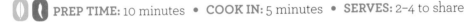 **PREP TIME:** 10 minutes • **COOK IN:** 5 minutes • **SERVES:** 2–4 to share

1 tbsp of peanut oil

2 cloves of garlic, crushed and finely chopped

1 tbsp of peeled and grated ginger root

1 red chili, seeded and finely chopped

1 tbsp of fermented salted black beans, rinsed and crushed

12 oz mixed oriental mushrooms (such as shimeji, oyster, and shiitake), sliced

1 tbsp of Shaohsing rice wine or dry sherry

1 scallion, finely chopped

FOR THE SAUCE

⅔ cup cold vegetable stock

1–2 tbsps of light soy sauce

1 tbsp of cornstarch mixed with 1 tbsp water

1. Heat a wok over high heat until it starts to smoke and then add the peanut oil. Add the garlic, ginger, chili, and crushed black beans and stir-fry for a few seconds. Toss in the mushrooms and stir together, then add the rice wine or dry sherry and stir for a few seconds.

2. Add the ingredients for the sauce and bring to a boil. As the sauce thickens, stir in the scallion, then transfer to a serving dish and serve immediately with jasmine rice.

Light choy sum with oyster sauce

Choy sum ("vegetable heart" in Cantonese) is a popular leafy vegetable that is also known as flowering cabbage because of the yellow flower the plant produces. The leaves and stem are both tender when cooked and provide a sweet, mild flavor. It can be blanched and added to soups, as well as stir-fried or steamed.

PREP TIME: 5 minutes • **COOK IN:** 3 minutes • **SERVES:** 2–4 to share

Large bunch of choy sum

2 tbsps of vegetarian oyster sauce

Bring a large saucepan of water to a boil, then add the choy sum and blanch for 2–3 minutes. Drain in a colander and transfer to a serving plate, then drizzle over the oyster sauce (the residual heat from the cooked leaves will heat up the sauce) and serve immediately.

Pickled salad

I love pickled Chinese vegetables, especially as an appetizer, as they help to "wake" the taste buds. This is a simple dish that works well as an accompaniment to a spicy main dish, giving cooling relief. It is also delicious as a topping on *gua bao* (see page 171).

PREP TIME: 10 minutes, plus 20 minutes for chilling • **SERVES:** 2–4 to share

½ cucumber (unpeeled), seeded and very thinly sliced

1 carrot, thinly sliced on the diagonal

6 small radishes, thinly sliced

1 tbsp of mirin

3 tbsps of clear rice vinegar or cider vinegar

1 tsp of superfine sugar

¼ tsp of coarse sea salt

Add all the ingredients to a large bowl, then toss together, cover with plastic wrap, and chill in the fridge for 20 minutes before serving.

Fish-fragrant eggplant with tofu

This is an adaptation of one of my favorite Sichuan dishes. It doesn't actually contain any fish but is called "fish-fragrant" or *yu xiang* because of the stock it is cooked in. (See also Fish-Fragrant Eggplant with Pork on page 115.) You can use standard Western eggplant for this dish, but if you can, try to get hold of the long Asian variety, which is sweeter and more tender. The traditional way of cooking the eggplant is to deep-fry it in oil and then stir-fry with the remaining ingredients, but this version is healthier and works just as well in my opinion.

PREP TIME: 10 minutes • **COOK IN:** 8 minutes • **SERVES:** 2–4 to share

2 tbsps of peanut oil

1 eggplant, sliced into batons

2 cloves of garlic, crushed and finely chopped

1-inch piece of fresh ginger, peeled and grated

1 red chili, seeded and finely chopped

1 tbsp of chili bean sauce

7 oz fresh firm tofu, drained and cut into ½-inch cubes

1 scallion, thinly sliced

FOR THE SAUCE

7 tbsps of cold vegetable stock

1 tbsp of light soy sauce

1 tbsp of Chinkiang black rice vinegar or balsamic vinegar

1 tbsp of cornstarch mixed with 1 tbsp of water

1. Heat a wok over high heat until it starts to smoke and then add half the peanut oil. Add the eggplant and stir-fry until browned, then cook, still stirring, for 5 minutes or until softened. During this process, keep adding small drops of water to create a little steam to help soften the eggplant as it cooks. Transfer to a plate and set aside.

2. Place the wok back over high heat and add the remaining peanut oil. Add the garlic, ginger, chili, and chili bean sauce and cook together for a few seconds. Add the cooked eggplant, followed by all the ingredients for the sauce, then add the tofu and bring to a boil.

3. Cook until the sauce has thickened and then stir in the scallion. Remove from the heat and serve immediately with jasmine rice.

> **ALSO TRY**
> I like using fresh firm tofu in this dish, as it soaks up the flavors and adds protein, but if you are not a fan of tofu, you could substitute shiitake mushrooms or chestnut mushrooms instead.

Special mixed vegetables

I rarely buy prepared vegetables, but there is a place for them. I recently stumbled across a packet of assorted baby corn, mini broccoli florets, peas, and grated carrots and I was most impressed with the quality and freshness. This sort of selection comes in very handy as an addition to quick-fried rice. It also makes a great accompaniment to other dishes. Fast, easy, delicious, and nutritious, it could be served as an alternative to rice as part of a low-carb meal.

PREP TIME: 5 minutes • **COOK IN:** 4 minutes • **SERVES:** 2–4 to share

1 tbsp of peanut oil

1 tbsp of peeled and finely grated fresh ginger

11 oz prepared mixed vegetables (such as baby corn, broccoli florets, peas, and grated carrots)

1 tbsp of light soy sauce

1 tbsp of toasted sesame oil

Pinch of ground white pepper

Heat a wok over high heat until it starts to smoke and then add the peanut oil. Add the grated ginger and stir for a few seconds, then add the mixed vegetables and cook for 2 minutes, stirring constantly. Add a small dash of water to create some steam and help soften the vegetables, then season with the soy sauce, toasted sesame oil, and white pepper and serve immediately.

ALSO TRY
For a more substantial vegetarian meal, you could add pieces of smoked marinated deep-fried tofu.

Buddha's stir-fried mixed vegetables

There are many variations on this classic dish, familiarly known as "Buddha's delight," and traditionally it would also contain such ingredients as dried lily bulbs and straw mushrooms. This is my take on the dish. You can buy the wood ear mushrooms in a Chinese supermarket; if you can't find them, you can omit them, but they are worth seeking out because they are so versatile. They can be used in salads, soups, stir-fries, spring rolls, stews, and dumplings. They are mostly available dried and will need pre-soaking in warm water before using. As they rehydrate, they double in size and can then be sliced before being added to whatever dish you're making. They have a bland taste but provide a great crunchy texture, and this recipe wouldn't be the same without them.

PREP TIME: 15 minutes • **COOK IN:** 5 minutes • **SERVES:** 2–4 to share

1 tbsp of peanut oil

1 tbsp of peeled and grated fresh ginger

1 carrot, cut into matchsticks

Small handful of dried Chinese wood ear mushrooms, soaked in hot water for 20 minutes, drained, and sliced

Small handful of baby corn, sliced lengthwise

One 8-oz can of bamboo shoots, drained and cut into matchsticks

Small handful of bean sprouts

2 scallions, thinly sliced

FOR THE SAUCE

7 tbsps of cold vegetable stock

1 tbsp of light soy sauce

1 tbsp of vegetarian oyster sauce

1 tsp of toasted sesame oil

1 tbsp of cornstarch

1. Heat a wok over high heat until it starts to smoke and then add the peanut oil. Add the grated ginger and stir-fry for a few seconds. Add the carrot, mushrooms, baby corn, and bamboo shoots and stir-fry for 2 minutes.

2. Meanwhile, mix all the sauce ingredients together in a small bowl.

3. Add the sauce to the wok and bring to a boil. When the sauce has thickened, reduce the heat, then add the bean sprouts and scallions and cook for 1 minute. Transfer to a serving plate and serve with jasmine rice.

Mock duck and tender stem broccoli stir-fry

A Chinese menu has much to offer a vegetarian thanks to the abundance of assorted ingredients made predominantly from soy and wheat gluten, including mock pork, mock duck, mock chicken, and even mock tuna and swordfish! When added to dishes that would normally contain meat, these substitutes can easily fool you, as they taste like the real thing. I recently had a Kung Po "chicken" dish, only to be told it wasn't made with chicken. You may be able to find some canned varieties in a Chinese supermarket. If you can't, then use vegetarian sausages, sliced up, instead.

PREP TIME: 15 minutes • **COOK IN:** 5 minutes • **SERVES:** 2–4 to share

2 tbsps of peanut oil

1 clove of garlic, crushed and finely chopped

1 tbsp of peeled and grated fresh ginger

1 red chili, seeded and finely chopped

4 shiitake mushrooms, sliced

One 8-oz can of mock duck, rinsed, drained, and sliced

3½ oz peeled broccoli stems, sliced on the diagonal

3½ oz green beans, topped and tailed

2 tbsps of vegetarian oyster sauce

1 tbsp of light soy sauce

Pinch of light brown sugar

Pinch of ground white pepper

Dash of toasted sesame oil

1. Heat a wok over high heat until it starts to smoke and then add the peanut oil. Add the garlic, ginger, chili, and mushrooms and stir-fry for 1 minute, then add the mock duck and stir-fry for just under a minute. Add the broccoli and green beans and stir-fry for an additional minute.

2. Season with the remaining ingredients, then remove from the heat and serve immediately with boiled rice.

Specials

In Taiwan, whenever there was a special occasion, my grandmother would spend days in advance preparing the food for it and she would go to town creating a whole range of dishes, whether meat, fish, or vegetarian, as well as noodles and desserts—every chapter in this book!

Preparations for the Dragon Boat Festival or *Duan Wu Jie* in Mandarin Chinese—which falls on the fifth day of the fifth month in the lunar calendar and celebrates the life of the legendary poet Chu-Yuan—were a particular labor of love for her. During the festival, a special type of rice dumpling wrapped in bamboo leaves, *zong-zi*, is eaten, and my grandmother would make hundreds of these for the family to enjoy.

Just selecting the ingredients for them seemed to take forever. A week before, my grandfather would be dispatched to pick the best dried Chinese mushrooms from the market, along with the freshest shallots and ginger. Then my grandmother and great-aunts would set to work preparing all the ingredients for the rice parcels. Hours would be spent soaking the dried mushrooms and you could hear the sound of shallots being endlessly chopped in the days leading up to the festival. Pork belly would be stewed for hours, "red-cooked" style, with star anise, soy sauce, and sugar, until the meat was meltingly tender. Meanwhile, large bamboo steamers full of salted duck-egg yolks would be cooking away on a wooden stove nearby.

All these ingredients would be wok-fried, together with seasoned raw rice, then wrapped in bamboo leaves and steamed for hours until the rice was soft and slightly sticky. When the time finally came, we would devour the dumplings within minutes! I now appreciate all that effort far more than I did as a child.

These days, whenever a family friend gives me some homemade *zong-zi*, I eat them with wholehearted appreciation because I know just how much labor has gone into making them.

Specials are just that—special. There is nothing more satisfying than seeing your guests enjoy the food you have prepared for them, and nothing more delightful than when someone cooks for you. Happy memories such as these are gold dust: they will touch your heart and stay with you always.

The recipes that follow include some of my favorite special-occasion dishes that I like to serve for family and friends. Some Chinese takeout shops serve special dishes, but I notice that most of these are Southeast Asian in origin, such as Thai green chicken curry or Malaysian-style ho fun rice noodles. I would like the specials section to be more varied and offer some Chinese street food as well as "fu-sian" dishes.

In my fantasy takeout shop, I would include dishes such as my Chili Bean Braised Beef with Cilantro and Steamed Mantou, Spiced Lamb Chops with Pickled Onion and Cilantro Salad, or "Tiger Bites Pig" (Chinese Hamburgers) with Pickled Cucumber made with Hakka-Style Pork Belly (see pages 162, 175, and 171). These dishes are also perfect for entertaining and don't take too long to prepare. There is a recipe for every occasion here, whether casual or more formal. And they can easily be doubled for larger gatherings for sharing, along with some simple side dishes.

Chili bean braised beef with cilantro and steamed mantou

Stewed dishes are in my opinion perfect winter food. I love the tantalizing flavor of slow-cooked beef with soy and chili bean sauce, so I adapted my Taiwanese-style beef noodles to make a quicker version—a lifesaver for a last-minute dinner party. This dish is served with fluffy *mantou*, which can be bought from Chinese supermarkets and steamed from frozen. Slightly sweet in taste, these wheat-flour buns are ideal for soaking up the spicy sauce—a perfect balance of flavor and texture.

PREP TIME: 10 minutes • **COOK IN:** 20 minutes • **SERVES:** 2–4 to share

4 frozen *mantou* buns
1 tbsp of peanut oil
2 large shallots, chopped
12 oz beef sirloin, cut into ½-inch cubes
1 tbsp of Shaohsing rice wine or dry sherry
2 scallions, sliced
1 tbsp of chili oil (optional)
Handful of cilantro, roughly chopped

FOR THE SAUCE
7 tbsps of beef stock
2 tbsps of chili bean paste
2 tbsps of light soy sauce
1 tsp of dark soy sauce
1 tsp of light brown sugar
1 tbsp of honey

> **ALSO TRY**
> You could also use stewing beef and slow-cook it. If you can't get hold of *mantou*, serve with buttered rolls instead.

1. Place the *mantou* in a bamboo steamer lined with wax paper. Set the steamer over a saucepan of boiling water (making sure the bottom of the steamer doesn't touch the water) and steam for 15–20 minutes, or until the buns are soft and heated through. Reduce the heat to low and keep the *mantou* in the steamer until ready to serve.

2. Meanwhile, heat a wok over high heat until it starts to smoke and add half the peanut oil. Stir-fry the shallots for 2 minutes, or until slightly softened. Scoop the shallots to one side of the wok, add the remaining peanut oil, and add the beef.

3. As the beef starts to brown, add the rice wine or dry sherry and stir-fry for 1–2 minutes, or until fully browned. Add the scallions and toss together with the beef, then add all the ingredients for the sauce and cook over medium heat for 12 minutes, or until the beef is tender.

4. Season with the chili oil (if using), stir in the chopped cilantro, and serve with the steamed *mantou*.

Crackling pork shoulder with Chinese spices

This is not your typical takeout dish, but in China, Hong Kong, and Taiwan you have takeout eateries that sell roast duck and roast pork, as well as various stewed meats, which you can buy and reheat or cook with at home. Most families don't make their own roast meat because they need special ovens and there are rotisseries that do the job just as well. However, I do love roasts, especially on a Sunday (no doubt influenced by my English friends). This one is really easy to cook, making for effortless, fuss-free entertaining. If I had a takeout shop, I would install gigantic ovens and roast whole ducks, chickens, and joints of pork like this one.

PREP TIME: 10 minutes, plus 15 minutes for resting • **COOK IN:** 40 minutes • **SERVES:** 4

1 lb 2 oz boneless pork shoulder

FOR THE SPICE MIX
2 tsps of sea salt
1 tbsp of black peppercorns
1 tbsp of light brown sugar
1 tbsp of Chinese five-spice powder
2-inch piece of cassia bark or cinnamon
4 cloves
2 star anise

1. Preheat the oven to 400°F.

2. Combine all the ingredients for the spice mix in a mortar and pound with a pestle into a fine powder. Alternatively, grind in a spice grinder, if you have one.

3. Score the surface of the pork fat with a sharp knife (this is to help keep the pork crisp during cooking), then rub the spice mixture over the pork, working it well into the score lines on the fatty side of the meat.

4. Place the pork in a roasting pan and roast in the oven for about 40 minutes, or until the juices run clear when the meat is pierced with a knife or skewer. Remove from the oven and allow to rest for 15 minutes before slicing. This tastes delicious with the Sweet Roasted Vegetables (see page 146).

Pork tenderloin with kimchi and enoki mushrooms

I had a delicious kimchi dish at a Japanese restaurant in Taiwan earlier this year. We had ordered far too much and at the end of the meal my sister-in-law put the leftovers aside to be boxed to take home, in the process marrying a stir-fried pork dish with some kimchi (Korean-style fermented vegetables). We had it as a late-night snack when we got back to her house later and ever since then I have been addicted to pork with kimchi. It pays to use a good-quality kimchi—you can buy it from a Chinese supermarket, either in a jar or in a foil pack from the chilled section. And don't forget the enoki mushrooms—they provide a delicious soft, chewy texture and soak up all the juices. If you can't get hold of them, however, just leave them out. This is a fast-wok dish: make sure you work quickly to avoid overcooking the pork tenderloin.

PREP TIME: 5 minutes • **COOK IN:** 5 minutes • **SERVES:** 2–4 to share

1 tbsp of peanut oil

1-inch piece of fresh ginger, peeled and sliced into matchsticks

2 pork tenderloins (11 oz in total), cut into ¼-inch slices

1 tbsp of mirin

1 tbsp of light soy sauce

7 oz kimchi

7 oz enoki mushrooms

2 pinches of sea salt

1 tbsp of clear rice vinegar or cider vinegar

2 scallions, sliced on the diagonal

Drizzle of chili oil

1. Heat a wok over high heat until it starts to smoke and then add the peanut oil. Stir-fry the ginger for a few seconds, then add the pork slices and stir-fry for 2 minutes or until browned at the edges.

2. Add the mirin and soy sauce and cook for 1 minute, then add the kimchi and enoki mushrooms. Season with the salt and vinegar and mix in well. Stir in the scallions and then drizzle over the chili oil and serve immediately with jasmine rice.

Chinese sweet pork sausages with garlic

Chinese pork sausages are traditionally made in the month before Chinese New Year when the winter sun dries the meat. My favorite are Taiwanese fresh *xiang chang* sausages, slightly sweet and perfect with boiled rice and stir-fried vegetables. There are several different varieties of sausage: red and white ones are made from pork belly, for instance, while darker ones include liver. You can buy them vacuum-packed from Chinese supermarkets—they keep for weeks in the fridge and can be frozen too. They shouldn't be eaten raw, however, and the best way to prepare them is to steam them.

In this recipe I've steamed the sausages, then pan-fried them and served them with slices of garlic. They could be served as an appetizer or as an accompaniment to a variety of dishes, such as the Fish-Fragrant Eggplant with Pork or Yellow Bean Chicken with Green Beans and Shiitake Mushrooms (see pages 115 and 78).

PREP TIME: 5 minutes • **COOK IN:** 20 minutes • **SERVES:** 2–4 to share

2 dried Chinese pork sausages

1 tbsp of peanut oil

2 cloves of garlic, very thinly sliced

3 sprigs of cilantro, to garnish

1. Place the sausages on a heatproof plate in a bamboo steamer, cover with the lid, and set over a saucepan or wok of boiling water. Steam for 15 minutes (making sure the bottom of the steamer doesn't touch the water), then remove from the heat and rest for 2 minutes in the basket. Take the sausages out of the steamer and cut on the diagonal into ¼-inch slices.

2. Heat a wok over high heat until it starts to smoke and then add the peanut oil. Add the slices of sausage and stir-fry for 2 minutes, then transfer to a serving plate, alternating the slices of sausage with the garlic. Serve immediately, garnished with the sprigs of cilantro.

ALSO TRY
You could try serving the sausage as they do in China, with the garlic on the side. The idea is to eat a slice of sausage with a slice of raw garlic.

Hakka-style pork belly

In traditional Hakka cuisine, this dish is known as *mei cai ko rou*. The meat is steamed with some fermented dried cabbage in a soy-flavored cooking liquid, which gives the dish a salty as well as sweet, earthy flavor. I like to serve the pork belly Western-style, with stir-fried savoy cabbage and mashed potatoes. Or you could always use it for making my Chinese-style "hamburger" on page 171.

PREP TIME: 10 minutes • **COOK IN:** 1¾ hours • **SERVES:** 4

3 pieces of pork belly (1 lb 7 oz in total), skin on

2 tbsps of peanut oil

1 tbsp of dark soy sauce

1-inch piece of fresh ginger, peeled and sliced into matchsticks

1 tbsp of Sichuan peppercorns

1 tsp of cornstarch mixed with 1 tbsp of water

FOR THE SAUCE

2 star anise

7 tbsps of vegetable stock

¼ cup light soy sauce

1 tbsp of Shaohsing rice wine or dry sherry

2 tsps of light brown sugar

> **ALSO TRY**
> If you're watching your waistline and prefer a leaner cut of pork, use pork loins instead of belly.

1. Bring a large saucepan of water to a boil and add the pork pieces. Bring back up to a boil, then reduce the heat and simmer for 30 minutes. Drain the pork and dry on paper towels.

2. Meanwhile, add all the ingredients for the sauce to a pitcher or bowl and stir together.

3. Heat a wok over high heat until it starts to smoke and then add half the peanut oil. Add the pork pieces and season with the soy sauce, then fry the meat for 1 minute on each side or until browned. Remove the pork and transfer to a heatproof dish that will fit inside a large bamboo steamer.

4. Place the wok back over high heat and add the remaining peanut oil. Add the ginger and Sichuan peppercorns and stir-fry for a few seconds and then add the sauce, bringing it to a boil. Remove from the heat and pour over the pork in the steamer.

5. Place the steamer over a pan of boiling water (making sure that the bottom of the steamer doesn't touch the water) and steam the pork in the sauce over medium heat for 1 hour.

6. Remove the meat from the steamer and pour the juices into a small wok or saucepan, bring to a boil, and then add the cornstarch paste to thicken the sauce. Cut the pork into 2-inch slices, pour over the sauce, and serve immediately.

"Tiger bites pig" (Chinese hamburgers) with pickled cucumber

Known as *gua bao* ("pork belly buns") in Taiwan, this dish also goes by the name of "Tiger Bites Pig" because the sliced bun looks like a tiger's mouth with a "pig" (or piece of pork belly) in it! *Gua bao* typically consists of Hakka-Style Pork Belly (see page 168) sandwiched in a steamed wheat-flour bun, sprinkled with ground peanuts and sugar, and served with salted fermented cabbage. For this version of the dish, I've simply replaced the fermented cabbage with pickled cucumbers and the *gua bao* buns with *mantou*.

Deliciously fluffy and sweet, *mantou* are usually eaten for breakfast but go really well in this recipe. You can buy them from the frozen section of a Chinese supermarket, although some specialty stores sell the actual *gua bao* buns, pre-sliced, if you'd like to try those instead.

PREP TIME: 10 minutes, plus 20 minutes for marinating • **COOK IN:** 15–20 minutes • **SERVES:** 4

5 tbsps of roasted peanuts

2 tbsps of granulated sugar

4 frozen *mantou* buns

4 slices of warm freshly cooked Hakka-Style Pork Belly (see page 168)

Small handful of chopped cilantro, to garnish

FOR THE PICKLED CUCUMBER

½ cucumber (unpeeled), halved lengthwise and thinly sliced

1 tbsp of clear rice vinegar or cider vinegar

1 tbsp of mirin

Pinch of salt

Pinch of brown sugar

1. Place all the ingredients for the pickled cucumber in a bowl, stir together, cover, and leave to marinate for 20 minutes. Put the peanuts in a mortar and crush with a pestle to a fine powder, or use a spice grinder, then mix with the sugar.

2. While the cucumber is marinating, place the *mantou* in a bamboo steamer lined with wax paper. Set the steamer over a saucepan of boiling water (making sure the bottom of the steamer doesn't touch the water) and steam for 15–20 minutes, or until the buns are soft and heated through.

3. Slice each bun in half, place a piece of pork belly inside, and drizzle over some of the cooking juices. Add some of the pickled cucumber, sprinkle over a little of the peanut and sugar mixture, and garnish with some chopped cilantro.

Roast pork brioche buns with caramelized red onions

These are ideal for children's parties and make a change from boring sandwiches. They would also be great for a summer barbecue. The pork can be marinated in advance and then quickly cooked and sandwiched in the brioche buns just before serving.

PREP TIME: 10 minutes, plus 20 minutes for marinating • **COOK IN:** 10 minutes • **SERVES:** 4

1 lb 2 oz pork tenderloin

1 tbsp of peanut oil

1 tbsp of honey

4 small brioche buns

4 Boston lettuce leaves

FOR THE MARINADE

1 clove of garlic, crushed and finely chopped

2 tbsps of yellow bean sauce

1 tbsp of Shaohsing rice wine or dry sherry

1 tbsp of light soy sauce

1 tbsp of peanut oil

FOR THE CARAMELIZED RED ONIONS

1 tbsp of peanut oil

1 red onion, thinly sliced

1 tbsp of light brown sugar

1. Put all the ingredients for the marinade into a large bowl and stir together. Add the pork tenderloin and turn in the mixture to coat, then cover and place in the fridge to marinate for at least 20 minutes.

2. Remove the pork from the marinade (reserving it) and cut into ¼-inch slices. Heat a wok over high heat until it starts to smoke and then add the peanut oil. Add the pork slices and stir-fry for 2 minutes.

3. Stir the honey into the marinade, then add to the pork and cook for another 2 minutes or until the meat has acquired a slightly sticky glaze. Transfer to a plate and leave to rest.

4. Meanwhile, make the caramelized red onions. Heat a small wok over medium-high heat until it starts to smoke and then add the peanut oil. Add the onion slices and cook for 3 minutes or until softened, then sprinkle over the sugar and cook for an additional 1–2 minutes or until sticky and caramelized.

5. Slice each bun in half, add a lettuce leaf, some fried pork slices, and a spoonful of caramelized onions and serve immediately.

Spiced lamb chops with pickled onion and cilantro salad

This dish takes its inspiration from the spices used by the Muslim Chinese in their cuisine. Their ancestors would have traveled to China along the Silk Road, bringing their own customs and cooking styles, including spicy lamb kebabs, which can now be purchased from food stalls and takeout shops across the country. I've taken my cue from them for this dish, in which the lamb is first marinated in a spice paste and then cooked in a wok. It's fast, simple, delicious, and healthy, as well as perfect for entertaining.

PREP TIME: 10 minutes, plus 20 minutes for marinating • **COOK IN:** 5 minutes • **SERVES:** 2

4 lamb chops
1 tbsp of peanut oil
Salt and ground white pepper

FOR THE SPICE PASTE
1 tbsp of peanut oil
2 green chilies, sliced
1 tsp of dried chili flakes
1 tsp of medium curry powder
1 tsp of turmeric
1 tsp of ground cumin
1 tbsp of Shaohsing rice wine
    or dry sherry

FOR THE SALAD
1 white onion, sliced into rings
Juice of ½ lemon
¼ cup clear rice vinegar or
    cider vinegar
1 tbsp of mirin
¼ tsp of salt
¼ tsp of superfine sugar
Small handful of cilantro,
    finely chopped

1. Place the onion rings for the salad in a bowl with the lemon juice and 2 cups of water and leave to marinate for 10 minutes.

2. Meanwhile, put all the ingredients for the spice paste in another bowl and mix together well. Add the lamb chops and turn in the paste to coat, then cover with plastic wrap and leave to marinate for 20 minutes.

3. Drain the onion rings well, then place in a clean bowl with all the remaining ingredients for the salad except the cilantro, stir together to combine, and set aside to marinate for 10–15 minutes. Sprinkle over the cilantro just before serving.

4. Heat a wok over high heat until it starts to smoke and then add the peanut oil. Add the marinated lamb chops and fry for 2 minutes on each side. (Fry for another 1–2 minutes if you prefer them well done.)

5. Season with salt and ground white pepper and serve with the pickled onion and cilantro salad.

Cantonese-style steamed lobster with ginger soy sauce

This recipe is inspired by the Cantonese way of serving steamed fish—lightly dressed in a hot ginger soy oil that allows the fresh sweet flavor of the fish to come through. I decided to try it with lobster and it works really well—perfect for a romantic dinner for two. Try serving it with stir-fried vegetables and some Egg and Asparagus Fried Rice (see page 186).

PREP TIME: 10 minutes, plus 30 minutes for chilling • **COOK IN:** 12 minutes • **SERVES:** 2

1 live lobster
2 scallions, sliced
   lengthwise
Handful of cilantro sprigs

FOR THE GINGER SOY SAUCE
2 tbsps of peanut oil
1 tbsp of peeled and grated
   fresh ginger
¼ cup light soy sauce
1 tbsp of toasted sesame oil

1. First place the lobster in the freezer for 30 minutes. Remove from the freezer and quickly slice through the head with a sharp knife, then slice the lobster in half lengthwise, reserving the head.

2. Lay the lobster halves shell side down on a heatproof plate and place inside a large bamboo steamer. Cover the steamer with the lid and set over a wok or saucepan filled with boiling water, making sure the bottom of the steamer does not touch the water.

3. Steam over high heat for 10 minutes, then take off the heat. Remove the lid and drape the scallions and cilantro sprigs over the top of the lobster, then replace the lid to allow the herbs to wilt and soften in the steam. Keep the lobster in the steamer until ready to serve.

4. Next make the ginger soy sauce. Heat a small wok over high heat until it starts to smoke and then add the peanut oil. Add the ginger and stir-fry quickly for a few seconds, then add the soy sauce and toasted sesame oil and bring to a boil. Remove the wok from the heat.

5. Remove the lid from the steamer, pour the hot sauce over the lobster, and serve immediately in the bamboo steamer basket.

Clams and Chinese sausage with bean sprouts and scallions

I love clams and Chinese sausages, so I decided to pair the two and the result is a fragrant, sweet, and savory dish. The bean sprouts add texture and soak up the flavor of the gingery, winey sauce. Very Chinese in taste, it is good served with some plain boiled rice.

PREP TIME: 15 minutes • **COOK IN:** 7 minutes • **SERVES:** 2–4 to share

11 oz clams

1 tbsp of peanut oil

1-inch piece of fresh ginger, peeled and sliced into matchsticks

3½ oz cooked Chinese sausage (see page 167), cut into ¼-inch slices

1 tbsp of Shaohsing rice wine or dry sherry

7 tbsps of vegetable stock

1 tbsp of light soy sauce

1 tbsp of cornstarch mixed with 1 tbsp of water

Large handful of bean sprouts

1 scallion, cut on the diagonal into ½-inch slices

Sprig of cilantro, to garnish (optional)

1. First scrub the clams, removing any bits of debris from the shells and discarding any that remain open when tapped against a hard surface.

2. Heat a wok over high heat until it starts to smoke and then add the peanut oil. Add the ginger and stir-fry for a few seconds, then add the pieces of cooked Chinese sausage and stir-fry for a few seconds more. Add the clams and cook for 1 minute.

3. As the shells start to open, add the rice wine or dry sherry, then pour in the vegetable stock. Bring to a boil, then reduce the heat and cook for 3–4 minutes or until all the shells have opened. Discard any that remain closed.

4. Season with the soy sauce, then add the cornstarch paste, stir in the bean sprouts and scallion, and cook for 1 minute to allow the sauce to thicken. Transfer to a serving dish, garnish with a sprig of cilantro, if you like, and serve immediately.

Rice

Rice is the most important staple food for a huge proportion of the world's population. It is eaten all over the world and is cultivated in the continents of Asia, Australia, the Americas, and Africa. In China, we have a greeting, "*Ni chi fan le mei you?*" ("Have you eaten?" in Mandarin Chinese), in which the word "*fan*" means both "cooked rice" and "food." Not only is "rice" synonymous with "food," but as food and eating are at the forefront of people's minds, the word has evolved into part of a common everyday greeting!

In ancient China, wild rice first grew along the valleys of the fertile Yangtze River. It soon became domesticated and has been cultivated for thousands of years, with over 40,000 different varieties being grown. The most common form of rice is long grain, but there are also short-grain varieties, such as glutinous or sticky rice.

Many people ask me what is the best type of rice for Chinese cooking and I say just choose the one you like best. Long-grain rice like basmati is delicious, but for frying I prefer shorter-grained varieties that contain a bit more amylopectin, a type of starch that makes the rice stickier. My favorite is jasmine rice from Thailand, with its nutty-coconut aroma. I like to serve highly flavored dishes with jasmine rice. In my view, it makes the perfect accompaniment to many Chinese dishes. I mostly boil or steam it. I would only fry it to use up any leftover rice, and on the odd occasions when I have a craving for fried rice, I deliberately make more rice the night before to make sure I have plenty left over to cook with the next day. This is a technique I learned from my grandmother and mother—two kitchen gurus who could turn any leftovers, including rice, into the most amazing dishes.

I love the way freshly cooked rice grains, fluffy but still a bit al dente, absorb the flavors of dishes so well. As a child, I used to stain my rice with the sauces of my grandmother's dishes, whether it was a dressing made with oil, ginger, scallion, and chili or the dark-reddish sauce of red-cooked pig's trotters or Pork Rib, Turnip, and Carrot Broth with Cilantro (see page 34), a recipe handed down from my great-grandfather. (He had no teeth and would need to moisten the rice to make it into a watery congee so that it was easier for him to eat.)

The smell of jasmine rice cooking always reminds me of my grandmother's kitchen. I would know when it was time to eat when I could smell that delicate sweet fragrance in the air and hear the click of our Tatung rice cooker (my grandmother's favorite modern tool) switch from "cook" to "warm." My grandmother would then tell one of my great-aunts to fluff up the rice with an old bamboo spatula to "air" the grains before we formed a line to spoon it into our bowls.

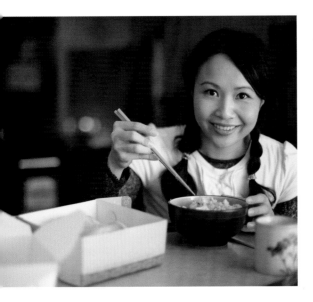

I have a huge extended family, and even though my grandparents lived on farmland, they were considered quite wealthy. (My grandfather always boasted that we were one of the first families in the village to own a fridge, rice cooker, and TV.) My grandfather is one of 11 siblings and together they own a bamboo farm, orangery, and a number of sweet potato patches. Since they all lived together, my great-aunts and great-uncles would eat together. Every mealtime was a banquet, with my grandmother at the helm as head chef with rotating sous-chefs, usually my second great-aunt, as she lived next door and was always on hand. Sometimes leftover rice from the dinner the evening before would be turned into congee for breakfast the next morning. My grandmother would heat up some water in her large wok on her wood-fired stove. Once the water "opened" (i.e., boiled), she would pour the rice in and stir, breaking it up in the hot water. She would boil the congee for a while until the starch from the rice broke down, creating a thick white porridge. Meanwhile, to accompany the congee, she would lay out small plates of mini pickled cucumbers, "stinky" fermented bean curd (*tofu ru* or *dao-ru* in Taiwanese) in soy sauce, pickled young tender bamboo shoots in chili oil, dried pork floss, salted fried red peanuts, and sheets of dried seaweed. She would also put out either boiled salted duck eggs or make fried eggs seasoned with soy sauce (see page 18 for my version of this dish!). Even now, in my Western kitchen, the smell of rice cooking transports me back to Taiwan and to memories of Pai He, a village found in the south of Taiwan.

Rice, however it's cooked, is a magical ingredient and to me much more than just an accompaniment. Cooked rice is also perhaps the most popular side dish on the takeout menu, especially in its fried form. With saltier or spicier dishes, I would usually recommend plain boiled rice or a light egg-fried rice like my Egg and Asparagus Fried Rice (see page 186). For lighter main dishes, you could serve a meatier fried rice, such as my version of Yangzhou Fried Rice (see page 188), which also makes a great brunch dish served on its own. However you like to serve rice, I hope there are a few dishes here to inspire you to try your own variations at home.

Boiled jasmine rice

In China and Taiwan, much of the rice that is cultivated is not exported. The variety used in Britain that is most similar to Chinese rice is jasmine rice, originally from Thailand. It is also a favorite of mine, with its fragrant, delicious aroma, and one of my staple pantry ingredients.

PREP TIME: 2 minutes • **COOK IN:** 15–20 minutes • **SERVES:** 4 to share

12 oz jasmine rice, rinsed until the water runs clear

Place the rice in a large heavy-bottomed saucepan and add 2½ cups of water. Bring to a boil, then cover with a tight-fitting lid, turn the heat down to low, and cook for 15–20 minutes or until all the water has been absorbed. Uncover the pan and remove from the heat. Fluff up the grains with a fork and serve immediately.

Fragrant star anise rice

When I was young, my grandmother often made "oiled" rice, a sticky rice moistened with soy pork drippings from pork cooked in star anise and soy sauce. When I am in search of those flavors, I cook the rice with some chicken or vegetable stock, in addition to the soy sauce and star anise, for a version that is lighter and healthier but still full of flavor and aroma.

(if using vegetable stock) **PREP TIME:** 5 minutes • **COOK IN:** 15–20 minutes • **SERVES:** 4 to share

12 oz jasmine rice, rinsed until the water runs clear
1¼ cups vegetable or chicken stock
1 star anise
1 tbsp of light soy sauce

Place the rice in a large heavy-bottomed saucepan and add the stock and 1 cup of water. Bring to a boil, add the star anise and soy sauce, then cover with a tight-fitting lid, turn the heat down to low, and cook for 15–20 minutes or until all the liquid has been absorbed. Uncover the pan and remove from the heat. Fluff up the grains with a fork and serve immediately.

Egg and asparagus fried rice

The first time I tried to make egg-fried rice, I made the mistake of frying rice that was freshly cooked and really moist. The result was a thick congealed porridge of egg and scallions—disaster! I was only 11 and so my father ate it anyway. To master fried rice, check that the wok is hot enough and use leftover cooked rice if possible. If using freshly cooked rice, make sure it's al dente rather than soft. Make sure there is enough oil in the wok too, and try not to stab at the rice but toss it in the wok as it fries. This is my classic egg-fried rice recipe, to which I like to add blanched sliced baby asparagus when in season, although frozen peas would work just as well.

PREP TIME: 5 minutes • **COOK IN:** 8 minutes • **SERVES:** 4 to share

3½ oz baby asparagus spears, woody ends snapped off

Salt and ground white pepper

1 tbsp of peanut oil

2 eggs, lightly beaten

12 oz cold leftover cooked jasmine rice or freshly cooked long-grain rice (see the tips below)

2 tbsps of light soy sauce

1 tbsp of toasted sesame oil

1 large scallion, thinly sliced

1. Blanch the asparagus spears in a saucepan of boiling salted water for 3 minutes, then drain and refresh in cold water. Slice the cooked asparagus crosswise into ¼-inch pieces and set aside.

2. Heat a wok over high heat until it starts to smoke and then add the peanut oil. Add the eggs and stir for 2 minutes to scramble, then add the rice and stir well in the wok to break it up. Add the blanched asparagus pieces and toss together well.

3. Season with the soy sauce, toasted sesame oil, and salt and pepper to taste. Add the scallion and mix well, then remove from the heat and serve immediately.

> **CHING'S TIPS**
> If cooking rice to use later, make sure the cooked rice is cooled for no longer than 30 minutes at room temperature, then transfer to a bowl or plastic container, cover, and keep refrigerated until ready to use. Only reheat/cook rice once after it has been cooked already.
>
> If using freshly cooked rice for a fried dish, try a long-grain variety such as basmati. For this dish, use 6 oz of uncooked long-grain rice (well rinsed) and boil in 1½ cups of water until all the water is absorbed. This will increase the cooking time by 20 minutes.

Ching's Yangzhou fried rice

This recipe from eastern China traditionally includes pieces of smoked Chinese ham, as well as egg, shiitake mushrooms, shrimp, and crabmeat. The result is a rich and elegant dish that has evolved into a Chinese takeout classic all over the world. When making it at home, I like the combination of Cantonese pork with baby shrimp and mixed vegetables, although you can vary this dish endlessly, using whatever vegetables you have on hand or just a handful of peas.

PREP TIME: 10 minutes • **COOK IN:** 5 minutes • **SERVES:** 2–4 to share

2 tbsps of peanut oil

3 eggs, beaten

2 oz cooked shelled baby shrimp

2 oz mixed vegetables (peas, mini broccoli florets, corn kernels, and grated carrot)

2 oz roast pork, diced

2 oz cooked chicken, shredded (optional)

14 oz cold leftover cooked jasmine rice (see the first tip on page 186) or freshly cooked long-grain rice (see the tip below)

2 tbsps of light soy sauce

2 tbsps of toasted sesame oil

Pinch of salt

2 pinches of ground white pepper

Sprigs of cilantro, to garnish (optional)

1. Heat a wok over high heat until it starts to smoke and then add half the peanut oil. Pour in the beaten eggs and leave to settle for 1–2 minutes, then swirl around the wok and, using a wooden spoon, stir the eggs to lightly scramble them. Transfer to a plate and set aside.

2. Reheat the wok and add the remaining peanut oil. Add the shrimp and mixed vegetables and stir-fry for less than 1 minute. Add the roast pork and cooked chicken (if using) and stir-fry for just under a minute. Add the cooked rice and mix well to break it down in the wok.

3. Return the scrambled eggs to the wok and season with the soy sauce, toasted sesame oil, salt, and pepper, then remove from the heat and serve immediately, garnished with cilantro sprigs, if you like.

> **CHING'S TIP**
> If using freshly cooked rice, take 7 oz of uncooked long-grain rice, such as basmati, rinse it well, and then boil in 1⅔ cups of water, cooking it until all the water has been absorbed. This will increase the cooking time by 20 minutes.
>
> **ALSO TRY**
> You could include other types of cooked meat in this dish, such as chunks of honey-roast ham instead of the chicken.

Chinese fruity roast duck and wild rice salad

When I was running my kitchen, I had to develop recipes all the time. There was one particular dish that was packed so full of flavor and was so popular with my customers that I had to share it here with you. It is my version of Chinese-style roast duck salad, to which I've added many twists, including a nutty soy dressing.

PREP TIME: 10 minutes, plus 40 minutes for cooling/chilling
COOK IN: 20–25 minutes • **SERVES:** 2–4 to share

7 oz brown basmati rice

3½ oz wild rice

11 oz roast duck (see page 68), shredded

1 cucumber (unpeeled), seeded and diced

1 red pepper, seeded and diced

Small handful each of pomegranate seeds, crushed walnuts, chopped dried apricots, and chopped dried cranberries

Small handful each of finely chopped cilantro leaves and finely shredded mint

2 scallions, thinly sliced

Handful of watercress and baby spinach leaves, to serve

FOR THE DRESSING

3 tbsps of extra-virgin olive oil

1 tsp of peeled and grated fresh ginger

2 tbsps of light soy sauce

1 tbsp of toasted sesame oil

1 tbsp of clear rice vinegar or cider vinegar

Pinch of salt and black pepper

1. Place both types of rice in a large heavy-bottomed saucepan and add 2½ cups of water. Bring to a boil, then cover with a tight-fitting lid, turn the heat down to low, and cook for 20–25 minutes or until the rice is al dente and all the water has been absorbed.

2. Uncover the pan and remove from the heat, then fluff up the grains with a fork and transfer to a bowl. Let the rice stand for 20 minutes to cool down, and then cover and refrigerate for at least 20 minutes, or preferably a few hours, until well chilled.

3. Shortly before serving, toss together all the remaining ingredients for the salad with the chilled rice in a large bowl. Place the dressing ingredients in a pitcher or bowl, stir well, and then add to the salad, tossing the salad ingredients together so that they are well coated. Serve on a bed of the watercress and baby spinach leaves.

Classic plain congee

Although in my family congee or rice porridge (*zhou* in Mandarin Chinese) is eaten mainly for breakfast or lunch, it can also be served for dinner. It doesn't usually feature on takeout menus in the West, but eateries in China regularly serve it for breakfast. If I had a takeout restaurant, I would serve congee in soup cartons as a restorative—it makes a great cure for hangovers and other ailments. Whenever I had an upset stomach, my grandmother would give me a steaming bowl of salted congee and I would feel I could live to see another day!

Congee traditionally consists of two types of short-grain rice, including some glutinous rice for a stickier, thicker consistency. If you have some glutinous rice in your pantry, then by all means include it as a fifth of the total quantity stated below. Otherwise using just jasmine rice will be fine.

PREP TIME: 5 minutes • **COOK IN:** 65 minutes • **SERVES:** 4–6 to share

9 oz jasmine rice or 7 oz jasmine rice mixed with 2 oz glutinous rice, rinsed until the water runs clear

1 cup vegetable stock

1. Pour the rice into a large heavy-bottomed saucepan, add the stock and 3 cups of water, and bring to a boil. Once boiling, reduce the heat to medium-low, place a tight-fitting lid on the pan, and cook for just over an hour, stirring occasionally to make sure the rice does not stick to the sides and the bottom of the pan, until the rice breaks down into a thick porridge.

2. Remove the pan from the heat and serve the congee plain as an accompaniment, or seasoned with a little salt if you have a stomachache!

> **CHING'S TIP**
> If you prefer a thinner, more watery porridge, simply add extra hot, boiled water as the rice cooks.
>
> **ALSO TRY**
> You can add all sorts of different ingredients to the congee once it's cooked, such as cooked green or split yellow mung beans or different types of meat and shellfish (see page 25 for a few ideas).

Noodles

I have always loved noodles. Dried noodles are one of my favorite pantry ingredients to reach for when hunger pangs strike and I need a quick fix. And I love noodles in whatever shape or form, whether made with rice or with wheat.

Noodles were always eaten in my family on birthdays. A birthday meal would consist of *misua*, very fine wheat-flour noodles (a bit like vermicelli) tossed in toasted sesame oil, garlic, and a little salt. When cooked, these noodles bundle up and stick together, and never break up unless you do the breaking; they are extremely fine and delicate, yet full of "spring" or "al-dente-ness."

In China, these uncut noodles symbolize longevity and that is why we eat them on festive occasions. It is my father's favorite dish, and whenever he has an upset stomach he asks for *misua*. The funny thing is that, having lived in England for all these years, my family would now buy a large cream cake to celebrate a birthday, but it would be reserved for dessert; we'd still have *misua* for the first course. A union of opposites, you might say: a simple savory dish followed by an extravagant pudding—so East and West.

If I had to choose between rice and noodles, it would have to be noodles. I am obsessed with them, even more so after running my own food business. In fact, it was my love of noodles that inspired me to set up Fuge. It was passing a sandwich chain serving bland wheat-flour noodles at £3.50 a box that showed me where my destiny lay. Life for me was not in a box of chocolates (to adapt a line from *Forrest Gump*) but a carton of *liang mein* ("cool noodles").

At the time, sushi had just taken off in Britain and I thought noodles might go down well too. I have always had a passion for *liang mein*, having bought it many times from snack stalls on the streets of Taipei: slippery chilled egg noodles served with grated carrots and cucumber in a spicy garlic and sesame dressing—that was my usual.

It was April 1999, my final year at university. While everyone else was applying for internships at large banks and accountancy firms, I picked up the phone and dialed all the supermarket chains I could, to try to book appointments with their buyers. I was desperate. After years of surviving by the skin of my teeth, I needed to turn my life around.

I tried making appointments with several supermarkets, including the one whose noodles I thought were awful, and they all turned me down except one—a small independent chain. I persuaded the buyer to book a meeting and showed up with a container of my homemade noodle salad, a few drawings, and an empty salad box. He asked me whether I had a kitchen, a health and hygiene certificate, distribution, product, pricing, marketing… To all these questions I said no. I could tell by the look on his face that he was not impressed.

But he took pity on me too, giving me a great long list of things I would need to set up in business. I wrote everything down and over the next few months, in the midst of studying for my finals, I gathered together all I would need and went back to him, having found a kitchen, three months' free rent, and a distributor just around the corner and with my first HACCP (Hazard Analysis and Critical Control Points) report. I could tell he wasn't expecting to see me, but he loved my "cool noodle" recipe and decided to give me a break.

At the beginning sales were poor—nobody wanted to eat noodles cold; people thought they should be heated. It was a hard time convincing customers, but I explained that if you eat pasta cold, in salads, the same principle can be applied to noodles.

I started experimenting with different types of noodles—udon, mung bean, buckwheat, and rice—and found suppliers who would provide them, and when orders went up I started importing my own range from Taiwan.

The business survived for nearly nine years thanks to the help and support of family, friends, and most of all my customers, who had a passion for good-quality noodles. I even ended up supplying the very people who first rejected my phone calls.

Those were very stressful times and for nearly ten years that was my life. I worked 12-hour days for six days a week; I would see buyers in the morning, then cook the products myself, boxing each dish individually with the help of a few staff. I worked like this for three years while building the business. Sometimes I look back and wonder how on earth I ever did it.

But treading that road has led me to where I am now. To think it all started with a box of take-out noodles…

Ching's life-changing Taiwanese liang mein

This is one of my favorite snacks. It should be garlicky, spicy, salty, and slightly vinegary—very refreshing when served cold on a hot summer's day.

PREP TIME: 10 minutes, plus 20 minutes for chilling • **COOK IN:** 4 minutes • **SERVES:** 2

5 oz dried white shi wheat-flour noodles or medium egg noodles

1 tbsp of toasted sesame oil

Large handful of bean sprouts (optional)

½ cucumber (unpeeled), seeded and grated

1 carrot, grated

Pinch of hot chili powder

FOR THE DRESSING

2 cloves of garlic, minced

2 tbsps of sesame paste or tahini

2 tbsps of light soy sauce

2 tbsps of clear rice vinegar or cider vinegar

1 tsp of chili sauce (optional)

1. Cook the noodles in a saucepan of boiling water for 2–3 minutes until al dente, or according to the instructions on the package. Drain, then rinse under cold running water and drain again. Drizzle with the toasted sesame oil and toss together to prevent the noodles from sticking to each other. Set aside to allow to cool.

2. Meanwhile, add the bean sprouts (if using) to another saucepan of boiling water and blanch for 30 seconds. Drain and refresh under cold running water, then set aside.

3. On two plates, arrange the salad ingredients in layers—noodles, grated cucumber, grated carrot, and bean sprouts (if using)—then cover in plastic wrap and place in the fridge to chill for 20 minutes.

4. Just before serving, mix all the dressing ingredients together in a pitcher or bowl, then drizzle over the noodle salad and mix together well. Sprinkle with the chili powder and serve immediately.

Chicken chow mein

Chow mein—which means "stir-fried noodles"—is one of a large number of noodle dishes. Less familiar dishes might include *e-mein*, Cantonese-style noodles, served with a sauce, and *lo-mein*, containing vegetables and meat or seafood and also served with a sauce.

   Chicken chow mein is a takeout classic. It's also my favorite chow mein dish. This is my version of it, one that I find myself making again and again; it's so good, in fact, that I had to include it.

PREP TIME: 10 minutes • **COOK IN:** 10 minutes • **SERVES:** 2

5 oz dried yellow shi wheat-flour noodles or medium egg noodles

2 dashes of toasted sesame oil

11 oz skinless chicken breasts, sliced into strips

Dash of dark soy sauce

1 tsp of Chinese five-spice powder

1 tsp of chili sauce (optional)

1 tbsp of cornstarch

1–2 tbsps of peanut oil

1 red pepper, seeded and finely sliced

5 oz bean sprouts

1 large scallion, sliced lengthwise

2 tbsps of light soy sauce

Ground black pepper

1. Cook the noodles in a saucepan of boiling water for 2–3 minutes until al dente, or according to the instructions on the package. Drain, then rinse under cold running water and drain again. Drizzle with a dash of sesame oil and toss together to prevent the noodles from sticking to each other.

2. Place the chicken strips in a bowl and season with the dark soy sauce, five-spice powder, and chili sauce (if using). Mix well, then lightly dust the chicken strips with the cornstarch.

3. Heat a wok over high heat until it starts to smoke and add the peanut oil, then add the chicken pieces and stir-fry for 3–4 minutes or until the chicken is cooked through and golden.

4. Add the red pepper and stir-fry for 1 minute, then add the bean sprouts and scallion and stir-fry for 30 seconds. Stir in the cooked noodles and season with the light soy sauce, the remaining dash of toasted sesame oil, and some freshly ground black pepper. Divide the noodles between plates and serve immediately.

Char siu roast pork noodle soup

Cantonese-style roast pork, or *char siu*—literally "fork roast," from the traditional method of cooking strips of pork on long forks over an open fire—is just the best ingredient to have in the kitchen. If you have enough time on the weekend, it pays to roast pork in this way. You can then use it over the next few days for sandwiches or noodle soups such as this one.

PREP TIME: 10 minutes, plus 20 minutes for marinating • **COOK IN:** 20 minutes • **SERVES:** 2

2 pork tenderloins

7 oz dried udon (flat wheat-flour) noodles

1 tbsp of toasted sesame oil

2½ cups vegetable stock

2 small heads of bok choy, leaves separated

1 scallion, thinly sliced

2 small handfuls of bean sprouts

FOR THE MARINADE

2 cloves of garlic, finely chopped

1 tbsp of peeled and grated fresh ginger

2 tbsps of yellow bean sauce

2 tbsps of honey

2 tbsps of light soy sauce

2 tbsps of Shaohsing rice wine or dry sherry

½ tsp of dark soy sauce

2 tbsps of peanut oil

1. Put all the ingredients for the marinade into a bowl and stir to combine. Add the pork and turn to coat, then cover the bowl and leave to marinate for 20 minutes.

2. In the meantime, preheat the oven to 400°F.

3. Heat a grill pan or skillet over high heat, and when it begins to smoke, cook the pork for 2 minutes on each side or until the outside edges are glazed and sticky. Transfer the pork to a roasting pan and roast in the oven for 12 minutes. Leave to rest for 5 minutes and then slice.

4. Meanwhile, cook the noodles in a saucepan of boiling water for 2–3 minutes until al dente, or according to the instructions on the package. Drain, then rinse under cold running water and drain again. Drizzle with the toasted sesame oil and toss together to prevent the noodles from sticking to each other.

5. Pour the vegetable stock into a separate saucepan and bring to a boil. Add the bok choy leaves and sliced scallion and remove from the heat.

6. Divide the cooked noodles between two bowls, add a handful of bean sprouts to each bowl, and ladle over the soup stock with the bok choy leaves and scallion. Top with the sliced roast pork and serve immediately.

Singapore noodles

I used to think this was a lengthy recipe, but these days supermarkets have all the ingredients ready-made—from cooked chicken breast and shelled tiger shrimp to diced bacon, mixed shredded stir-fry vegetables, and even cooked vermicelli rice noodles. All you have to do is heat the wok, add the ingredients, and season them—it takes no time at all!

PREP TIME: 15 minutes • **COOK IN:** 7 minutes • **SERVES:** 2

2 tbsps of peanut oil

1 tbsp of peeled and grated fresh ginger

1 red chili, seeded and finely chopped

5 shiitake mushrooms, sliced

1–2 tbsps of turmeric

6 oz raw shelled and deveined tiger shrimp

3½ oz smoked bacon, cut into lardons

1 red pepper, seeded and sliced

1 carrot, cut into matchsticks

Handful of bean sprouts

3½ oz cooked chicken breast, shredded

9 oz dried vermicelli rice noodles, soaked in hot water for 10 minutes and drained

1 tsp of dried chili flakes

2 tbsps of light soy sauce

2 tbsps of oyster sauce

1 tbsp of clear rice vinegar or cider vinegar

1 egg, beaten

Dash of toasted sesame oil

2 scallions, sliced lengthwise

1. Heat a wok over high heat until it starts to smoke. Add the peanut oil and stir-fry the ginger, chili, mushrooms, and turmeric for a few seconds.

2. Add the shrimp and stir-fry for 1 minute, or until they start to turn pink, then add the bacon and cook for less than 1 minute. Add the rest of the vegetables and cook for an additional minute, then add the cooked chicken and stir well to combine.

3. Add the noodles and stir-fry for 2 minutes, then season with the chili flakes, soy sauce, oyster sauce, and vinegar, and stir to combine.

4. Add the beaten egg, stirring gently until the egg is cooked through (just under a minute), and then season with the toasted sesame oil. Sprinkle with the scallions and serve immediately.

ALSO TRY
Instead of the bacon lardons, you could use diced Char Siu Roast Pork (see page 198), adding it with the shredded cooked chicken.

Ching's zha jiang noodles

Zha jiang ("fried sauce") noodles are a street-hawker snack, consisting of wheat-flour noodles mixed in a meat sauce. There are many different regional variations, however. In Sichuan, for example, they spice up the dish with Sichuan peppercorns or dried chilies. In Taiwan, they serve the noodles in a little broth with baby leeks or scallions. My mother likes to add pork and bamboo shoots.

 I came to make my own version, using leftovers I had in the fridge. Here I've mixed the noodles with ground beef, a green pepper, some shiitake mushrooms, and a few pantry ingredients. Hope you enjoy it!

PREP TIME: 10 minutes • **COOK IN:** 10 minutes • **SERVES:** 2–4 to share

7 oz dried white shi wheat-flour noodles or medium egg noodles

1 tbsp of toasted sesame oil

1 tbsp of peanut oil

2 cloves of garlic, crushed and finely chopped

14 oz ground beef

1 tbsp of Shaohsing rice wine or dry sherry

1 green pepper, seeded and diced

5 shiitake mushrooms, diced

One 14-oz can of chopped tomatoes

1 tbsp of light soy sauce

1 tbsp of chili oil

Pinch of sea salt

Pinch of ground white pepper

Handful of chopped cilantro, plus a few sprigs to garnish

1 scallion, thinly sliced, to garnish

1. Cook the noodles in a saucepan of boiling water for 2–3 minutes until al dente, or according to the instructions on the package. Drain, then rinse under cold running water and drain again. Drizzle with the toasted sesame oil and toss together to prevent the noodles from sticking to each other.

2. Heat a wok over high heat until it starts to smoke and add the peanut oil. Add the garlic and stir-fry a few seconds, then add the ground beef. Break the beef up in the wok, and as it starts to turn brown, pour in the rice wine or dry sherry.

3. Add the green pepper and mushrooms and stir-fry for 1 minute. Add the canned tomatoes and bring to a boil. Season with the soy sauce, chili oil, salt, and pepper and stir in the chopped cilantro. Remove from the heat and serve ladled on top of the noodles, garnished with the scallion and cilantro sprigs.

Shrimp and yellow bean chow mein with bok choy

Quick, tasty, and nutritious, this makes a great midweek supper. The yellow bean paste is a great pantry ingredient, perfect for marinades and speedy home-cooked meals like this one.

PREP TIME: 5 minutes • **COOK IN:** 7 minutes • **SERVES:** 2

3⅓ oz medium egg noodles

2 tbsps of toasted sesame oil

1 tbsp of peanut oil

1 large clove of garlic, crushed and finely chopped

1 red chili, seeded and finely chopped

7 oz cooked shelled and deveined tiger shrimp

3½ oz baby bok choy leaves

FOR THE SAUCE

1 tbsp of yellow bean paste

1 tbsp of light soy sauce

1 tbsp of Shaohsing rice wine or dry sherry

1 tbsp of cornstarch

1. Cook the noodles in a saucepan of boiling water for 2–3 minutes until al dente, or according to the instructions on the package. Drain, then rinse under cold running water and drain again. Drizzle the drained noodles with half the toasted sesame oil and toss together to prevent them from sticking to each other.

2. Meanwhile, mix together all the ingredients for the sauce, along with 7 tbsps of water, and set aside.

3. Heat a wok over high heat until it starts to smoke and then add the peanut oil. Add the garlic and stir-fry for a few seconds, then add the chili and fry for a few seconds more.

4. Add the shrimp, bok choy, and the sauce, then bring to a boil. Add the cooked noodles and toss together, then drizzle with the remaining toasted sesame oil and serve immediately.

> **ALSO TRY**
> For a vegetarian version of this dish, substitute sliced deep-fried tofu or shiitake mushrooms for the shrimp.

Crayfish sweet chili noodles

This is another of my favorite noodle salads, a dish that I made for one of my customers when I was running my food business. Herby, tangy, sweet, and spicy, this recipe is healthy and nutritious too.

PREP TIME: 15 minutes, plus 30 minutes for chilling • **COOK IN:** 3 minutes • **SERVES:** 2

7 oz dried yellow shi wheat-flour noodles or medium egg noodles

1 tbsp of toasted sesame oil

2½ oz mixed greens (such as watercress, arugula, and baby spinach)

8 snow peas, thinly sliced lengthwise

2 scallions, thinly sliced

½ red pepper, seeded and thinly sliced

10 sprigs of mint

Small handful of cilantro

3½ oz cooked crayfish tails in brine, drained

Lime wedges, to serve (optional)

FOR THE DRESSING

Juice of ½ pink grapefruit (including pulp)

2 tbsps of sweet chili sauce

1 tbsp of extra-virgin olive oil

1 scallion, finely chopped

Small handful of cilantro, finely chopped, plus extra to garnish

1. Cook the noodles in a saucepan of boiling water for 2–3 minutes until al dente, or according to the instructions on the package. Drain, then rinse under cold running water and drain again. Drizzle with the toasted sesame oil and toss together to prevent the noodles from sticking to each other. Transfer to a bowl, cover with plastic wrap, and place in the fridge to chill for 20 minutes.

2. Toss the chilled noodles with the remaining salad ingredients. Divide between two bowls, then cover with plastic wrap and place in the fridge to chill for an additional 10 minutes.

3. Just before serving, mix together the ingredients for the dressing, then pour over the salad, garnish with cilantro, and serve immediately with the lime wedges (if using).

Dessert

When I was little and growing up in Taiwan, the only sweet treat my brother and I had to look forward to was Yakult or *nian gao* ("sticky cake") at Chinese New Year. We didn't have any sweets or desserts otherwise. Dessert was usually in the form of sweetened soups like red bean soup, green bean soup with ginger and rock sugar, or *pai mu er* (white ear fungus soup with lotus nuts). Occasionally, we were treated to ice pops by our great-grandfather, who had a sweet tooth and would buy them for us. The flavors were nothing like those you would find in a Western shop, however. They would include corn, red kidney bean, green mung bean, black sesame, peanut, and taro—in fact, most of them were made from seeds or vegetables. But they were delicious. Whenever I return to Taiwan, I always hunt these out because they remind me so much of my childhood. I once had such a craving for them that I made my own red kidney bean and vanilla ice cream and, if I do say so myself, it was rather good. I urge you to try it sometime.

It was not until my family moved to South Africa that I encountered "proper" sweets and desserts. At school we had little plastic tubs of Nutella—I thought I had died and gone to heaven when I first tried one! Then there was the toffee-coated popcorn and sponge pudding…

Although I was exposed to sweet dishes at school, they were never featured on the menu at home. My mother would always make sure we had a plate or small bowl of fruit after dinner and it was the closest we got to dessert. Hence growing up I was always more of a "savory" than a "sweet" person.

It all changed when I first arrived in London. I remember taking a rather challenging exam, and before I knew it, I had been accepted to Mount School in North London. I was only 11 and things seemed very strange and new to me. Everyone kept asking if I was from Australia. I didn't know where Australia was—it was as foreign to me as my South African accent was to my schoolmates. Everyone said "Yeah" and I said "Jah." At the Mount, I was exposed to English food, English comfort food. I remember my first apple crumble with custard—it was so good, I nearly licked the bowl clean! At first, I brought packed lunches to school, but after a few weeks I looked forward to school lunch with a passion, and it was the dessert menu that I had my eye on.

Desserts would consist of apple pie, rhubarb crumble, spotted dick, sticky toffee pudding, chocolate pudding, bread and butter pudding, treacle pudding, jam roly poly, trifle, and Eton mess…I was in heaven. I couldn't understand why all the other girls hated school dinners so much. (I suspected it was more to do with trying to look cool.)

We didn't study home economics at school, but I did learn a little about French cooking. Our French teacher went by the name of Madame Wheeler and she was quite a character and rather hot-tempered. Luckily, I always did as I was told so I was mostly in her good books. Other girls were not so lucky, like Emily—poor Emily. Madame Wheeler would go around the classroom asking us questions individually. If you got the answer wrong or mispronounced a word, she would quickly lose patience. One day she was so incensed by Emily's failure to pronounce a word properly that she shrieked at her: "It's DEEEEEmanche, Emiiiily, DEEEEEEmanche!!!" I can remember very few words in French, but I'll never forget that one! Anyway, one week Madame Wheeler gave us an assignment to bake a French dessert called clafoutis. She wanted to immerse us in French culture. So we all went home and cooked our own version of the dish and brought it to school. It was a great recipe—the dark, sweet, slightly sour cherries were so delicious—and the best lesson I had ever had. After that, Madame Wheeler became my favorite teacher—I thought she was God!

I enjoy eating desserts more than I do cooking them, I have to admit. When I entertain, I cook Chinese and I like to go to town on the savory dishes, but when it comes to dessert, I usually knock up something quick and simple. It's not just to do with personal preference, however. Because Chinese dishes can be quite strong in flavor, I like to counterbalance them with something light and refreshing. These desserts are by no means the only ones in my repertoire, but I prefer to rely on recipes that don't take long to make or can be prepared in advance to save stress and give me more time with my guests.

Takeout shops don't normally feature desserts, so I have taken a bit of creative license here, although they would certainly feature on the menu of my fantasy takeout shop. I would serve tubs of homemade ice cream, like the Mango Ice Cream included here (see page 217), in addition to my Banana Toffee Fritters and Plum, Apple, and Lychee Spring Rolls in Cinnamon Sugar (see pages 215 and 212). At Chinese New Year, I would serve my customers slices of celebratory Nian Gao (see page 220) with small tubs of crème caramel or sticky toffee dipping sauce. The possibilities are endless!

Mango and coconut pudding with orange cinnamon syrup

I love mango pudding—it makes the perfect summer dessert. If you find yourself craving this when mangoes aren't in season and therefore not at their best, just use canned ones instead.

PREP TIME: 10 minutes, plus 1 hour for chilling/setting • COOK IN: 3 minutes • SERVES: 4

15 oz fresh mangoes or canned mangoes plus syrup

2 cups canned coconut milk

3½ oz superfine sugar

One 20 g packet of sheet gelatin, soaked in water and then squeezed

FOR THE ORANGE CINNAMON SYRUP

¼ cup dark corn syrup

¼ cup freshly squeezed orange juice

Juice of ½ lemon

1 star anise

TO SERVE

12 raspberries

4 sprigs of mint

1 small bowl of crushed pistachios (optional)

1. Puree the mango (including the syrup if using canned mangoes) in a blender. Transfer to a bowl and add the coconut milk and sugar, then mix well to dissolve the sugar.

2. In a liquid measuring cup, measure ¼ cup of hot water and add the soaked gelatin. Stir well to dissolve, then add to the mango and coconut puree and mix well.

3. Ladle the mixture into individual dishes, then place on a tray, cover with plastic wrap, and leave in the fridge for at least 1 hour to chill and set.

4. Meanwhile, to make the orange cinnamon syrup, place all the ingredients in a small saucepan and bring to a boil to infuse the flavors. Stir well and then set aside to cool to room temperature before covering and transferring to the fridge to chill for 20 minutes.

5. When ready to serve, pour 2 tbsps of the syrup over each pudding, decorate each with 3 raspberries and a sprig of mint, and allow your guests to sprinkle some crushed pistachios over the top.

Plum, apple, and lychee spring rolls in cinnamon sugar

This is a delicious late summer/early autumn dessert. Tart apples, juicy soft plums, and sweet lychees are fried in butter, cinnamon, and sugar and then wrapped in pastry and fried until crisp. They are delicious served with a scoop of vanilla ice cream.

PREP TIME: 15 minutes, plus 30 minutes for cooling
COOK IN: 5 minutes • **MAKES:** 12 small spring rolls

4 tbsps unsalted butter

1 apple, peeled and cored, then cut into ¼-inch cubes

2 oz ripe plums, pits removed, chopped into ¼-inch cubes

1 tsp of granulated sugar

1 tsp of ground cinnamon

2 oz fresh lychees, peeled and pits removed, or canned lychees, chopped into ¼-inch cubes

12 spring roll wrappers (6 inches square)

1 tbsp of cornstarch mixed with 1 tbsp of hot water

¾ oz superfine sugar

Vanilla ice cream, to serve

TO DECORATE
12 strawberries, stems left on
4 sprigs of mint

1. Heat a wok over medium heat and melt half the butter. Add the apple and plums and stir-fry for a few minutes until slightly softened. Add the granulated sugar and half the cinnamon and fry until the apples have a slight, sticky glaze, then stir in the lychees. Remove from the heat and allow the mixture to cool. (The filling can be made in advance, if you prefer.)

2. Take a spring roll wrapper and place it with one of the corners facing you so that the square forms a diamond. Place 1 tbsp of the fruit filling in the center of the pastry, then brush each corner with some of the cornstarch paste.

3. Bring together the two side corners of the "diamond" so that they meet over the filling, then bring the bottom corner up over the filling and continue rolling up to the top corner. Dab the top corner with more cornstarch paste and press lightly to secure the spring roll. Continue filling the remaining wrappers until you have made 12 in total.

4. Heat a wok over medium heat and melt the remaining butter. Place the spring rolls in the pan and fry for 1 minute, or until golden.

5. Place the superfine sugar and remaining cinnamon on a plate and carefully roll the spring rolls in the mixture. Decorate with the strawberries and sprigs of mint and serve with a scoop of vanilla ice cream.

Banana toffee fritters

I first had this in a Chinese restaurant in the UK. It is a classic, my favorite Chinese dessert, and some restaurants will use a combination of apples and bananas. This is just as delicious with canned jackfruit for a Southeast Asian twist, but bananas are my favorite.

PREP TIME: 10 minutes • **COOK IN:** 10 minutes • **SERVES:** 4 to share

2½ cups peanut oil
3 ripe bananas, plus 1 extra banana, sliced, to serve
4½ oz dark brown sugar
2 tbsps of white sesame seeds
Vanilla ice cream, to serve

FOR THE BATTER
4½ oz self-rising flour
2 eggs, beaten
Pinch of salt

CHING'S TIP
Take care not to overheat the sugar or it will taste burned, so keep the heat on medium-low when you are making the toffee coating for the fritters.

1. First make the batter for the fritters. Sift the flour into a bowl and stir in the beaten eggs, then gradually add 2 tbsps of water and mix together into a batter. Add the salt and leave to stand for a few minutes.

2. Place a wok over high heat and add the peanut oil. Heat the oil to 350°F, or until a cube of bread dropped in turns golden brown in 15 seconds and floats to the surface.

3. Peel the bananas, removing any strings from the fruit, and break each one into about 4 pieces. Dip the banana pieces one by one into the batter and then add to the hot oil. Fry for 3–4 minutes or until the pieces turn golden and float to the surface of the oil, then carefully remove from the oil with a slotted spoon and drain on paper towels.

4. While the banana fritters are draining, heat a small wok or skillet over medium heat and add the sugar. As the sugar starts to turn to liquid, quickly add the fritters and coat well in the caramelized sugar. Sprinkle over the sesame seeds as you turn the fritters in the pan: they will become toasted as they hit the hot sugar.

5. Remove the toffee fritters from the pan and dip them quickly in a bowl of iced water, then place on individual plates. Decorate with the banana slices and serve with a scoop of vanilla ice cream.

Pineapple and mango crunch trifle

My friends Lina and Alex came round one Sunday for lunch. I'd been dying to make them a special Chinese meal but had stayed up late the night before watching *Lawrence of Arabia* and then slept in, with no time to head to the supermarket. I pretty much had all the ingredients for lunch in my fridge except for dessert, so I had to improvise with whatever was on hand. Hunting around, I located a packet of Fox's Golden Crunch Creams, a pineapple, half a mango, some heavy cream, and a can of custard and, hey presto, this summery pudding was born (and it wasn't too bad either!).

PREP TIME: 10 minutes • **SERVES:** 4

10 crunchy vanilla-cream sandwich cookies, roughly chopped

7 oz peeled pineapple, cut into ½-inch cubes

7 oz peeled mango, cut into ½-inch cubes

Seeds from ½ pomegranate (optional)

4 tsps of Grand Marnier or pineapple or mango juice

1 cup store-bought vanilla custard

7 tbsps of heavy cream

Handful of raspberries, slices of strawberry, or pomegranate seeds, to decorate (optional)

FOUR SMALL TUMBLERS (ABOUT 9 OZ IN VOLUME)

1. Roughly chop up the cookies and divide among the four tumblers.

2. Arrange the fruit in layers in the glasses, then drizzle over the Grand Marnier or fruit juice and top each tumbler with a layer of custard. Whip the cream into soft peaks and spoon on top of the custard.

3. Decorate with raspberries, slices of strawberry, or a scattering of pomegranate seeds and serve.

Mango ice cream with exotic fruit

I love ice cream—but my favorite flavor is mango. This dessert can be prepared in advance and complements most savory dishes. It's cleansing and refreshing and perfect for a hot summer's day.

PREP TIME: 10 minutes, plus 1–7 hours for cooling/freezing
COOK IN: 2 minutes • **SERVES:** 4

2 large mangoes, peeled and pits removed, then sliced

3¼ cups heavy cream

3¼ oz superfine sugar

TO SERVE

2 mangoes, peeled and pits removed, then sliced

12 fresh lychees, peeled and pits removed, or canned lychees, sliced

4 large strawberries, hulled and sliced

Seeds of ½ pomegranate

1. Place the mangoes in a blender and whiz to a puree, then set aside.

2. Pour the heavy cream into a large saucepan placed over low heat and add the superfine sugar and the pureed mangoes. Mix well and then remove from the heat and set aside to cool. Once cooled, pour into an ice-cream machine and follow the instructions for making the ice cream.

3. To make the ice cream by hand, transfer the mixture to a freezer-proof container, cover, and place in the freezer for 2–3 hours, or until just frozen. Remove from the freezer and, using a fork or whisk, break up any ice crystals. Return to the freezer for an additional 2 hours, break up the ice again, then refreeze until solid. Just before serving, transfer the ice cream to the fridge to allow it to soften a little.

4. To serve, divide the sliced mangoes among individual dessert bowls. Add 2–3 scoops of the mango ice cream, then decorate with the lychee and strawberry slices and scatter over the pomegranate seeds.

Zesty fruit salad with star anise syrup

In the Chinese home, we usually have a plate of fruit for dessert. On special occasions my father would go to a Chinese supermarket and bring back a large pomelo, or Chinese grapefruit. Almost double the size of a Western grapefruit, this has a thick, pale green skin and opaque flesh. It's also less juicy than a Western grapefruit, which allows you to peel and segment the fruit more easily. My father would peel the pomelo in one piece so that my brother and I could pop it on our heads like a helmet! I like to serve this at Chinese New Year, with the orange segments signifying gold (or wealth) and the reddish color of the pomegranate seeds signifying good luck. Delicious and refreshing, with a hint of spice in the syrup, this makes a perfect dessert to follow a rich main course.

PREP TIME: 15 minutes, plus 20 minutes for chilling • **COOK IN:** 2 minutes • **SERVES:** 2

1 large pink grapefruit, peeled and segmented

2 small oranges, peeled and segmented

½ pomelo or 1 pink grapefruit, peeled and segmented

6 lychees, peeled and pits removed, or canned lychees

Seeds from ½ large pomegranate

FOR THE STAR ANISE SYRUP

¼ cup dark corn syrup

¼ cup freshly squeezed orange juice

2 star anise

¼ tsp of ground cinnamon

1. Mix together all the citrus fruit in a large bowl, cover with plastic wrap, and leave to chill in the fridge for 20 minutes.

2. Meanwhile, place all the ingredients for the syrup in a wok or saucepan and warm through over low heat, mixing well to combine and allow the different flavors to infuse. Remove from the heat and allow to cool, then cover and chill in the fridge for 20 minutes.

3. Just before serving, add the lychees to the citrus fruit, then divide the fruit between shallow dessert bowls. Drizzle over the chilled syrup and sprinkle over the pomegranate seeds, then serve immediately.

Nian gao

Nian gao, or "sticky cake," is traditionally served at Chinese New Year as a symbol of togetherness among families. *Nian* ("sticky") also means "year," while *gao* ("cake") can mean "high," to convey the sense that you rise "higher" each year. This is matched by the New Year saying *"Nian nian gao sheng"* ("Every year you rise in the ranks"), to indicate progress in your studies or career.

Nian gao consists of a sweetened dough made with glutinous rice flour. It is steamed and then left to cool and set. It's then dipped in batter and fried until the outside is crisp and the inside has melted to a sticky consistency, like marshmallow but denser. It is utterly delicious, and although the cake takes a bit of time to cook, it's very simple to make and you can prepare it in advance. My grandmother would cook it for us back in Taiwan, sometimes adding red beans or red Chinese dates to the cake mixture. This is my version of the dish, to which I've added just a hint of vanilla and a little wheat starch to make the dough less dense once it's cooked. Both glutinous rice flour and wheat starch can be bought from a Chinese supermarket.

PREP TIME: 10 minutes, plus 50 minutes for cooling/chilling
COOK IN: 65 minutes • **SERVES:** 4 to share

4½ oz light brown sugar
5 oz glutinous rice flour
1¼ oz wheat starch
1 tsp of vanilla extract
Peanut oil, for deep-frying

FOR THE BATTER
3½ oz potato flour
1 egg, beaten
Pinch of salt

ONE 8-INCH DIAMETER PIE PAN WITH 1¼-INCH SIDES

1. Fill a saucepan with ⅞ cup of water and bring to a boil. Remove from the heat, stir in the sugar until dissolved, and set aside to cool.

2. Sift together the rice flour and wheat starch into a bowl, then pour in the cooled sugar syrup and vanilla extract, and mix well to form a dough.

3. Line the pie pan with foil and pour in the cake mixture. Place the pan in a bamboo steamer set over a saucepan of boiling water (making sure the bottom of the steamer doesn't touch the water) and steam over high heat for 1 hour.

4. Remove the pan from the steamer and allow to cool to room temperature, then place in the fridge to chill and set for 30 minutes.

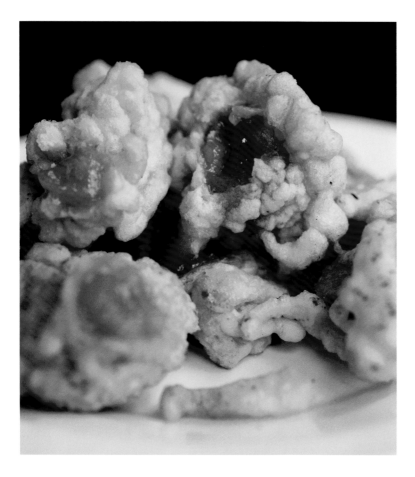

5. Just before serving, slice the cake into 1-inch pieces. Next make the batter by mixing together the potato flour with the beaten egg, salt, and 2 tbsps of water.

6. Place a wok over high heat and half fill it with peanut oil. Heat the oil to 350°F, or until a cube of bread dropped in turns golden brown in 15 seconds and floats to the surface.

7. Dip the cake pieces in the batter, then carefully lower into the hot oil and deep-fry for 5 minutes or until golden brown. Remove from the oil with a slotted spoon and drain on paper towels, then serve them hot on a plate so that everyone can help themselves.

Equipment

Woks

Buying and caring for your wok

There is nothing more traditional in Chinese cooking than using the wok. This great invention has been used for centuries to help feed millions of people all over the world. Woks come in various sizes and are made from different materials, so choosing one can be challenging. Traditional cast-iron woks are quite heavy and require seasoning, which is not too difficult. The wok comes coated with a film of oil; wash this off using a sponge and dishwashing liquid, then dry the wok over a high flame on the stove. Next, add a little oil to the wok (sesame oil is good because it burns quickly) and then use paper towels to rub in the oil over the entire wok, giving it a darkened, blackened effect. Once your wok is seasoned, don't use a metal scourer or steel wool on it, as you will take off the seasoning.

For those who prefer a lighter wok, I would recommend one made from carbon steel, which you season in the same way as the cast-iron wok. If you are new to wok cooking or just short on time, buy a nonstick wok made from carbon steel—it will require less oil for cooking than a cast-iron one, so it is healthier too.

When choosing your wok, make sure it feels comfortable and right for you. I prefer a one-handled wok with a medium handle that is not too thick to hold. In terms of size, choose a medium wok between 12 inches and 16 inches in diameter, which will hold a medium-sized bamboo steamer comfortably and allow you to cook enough to serve at least four.

For those who don't have a gas stove, I would say invest in a new stove! I find that electric stoves are just not right for wok cooking—you can buy a flat-bottomed wok, but you never really get enough heat to cook the food. However, you could invest in a good electric wok, which I have used and found not too bad.

Techniques for cooking in a wok

Stir-frying

The classic use of a wok—a touch of oil and lots of stirring—ensures that the ingredients keep their crunch and take on a smoky flavor. To help you cook your dish to perfection, however, there are a few things to observe.

1. Preparation

Always prepare the ingredients before you start, as you won't have time once you start cooking. Cut all the meat or fish to the same size—this ensures that the pieces cook in the same time. This principle also applies to vegetables. For leafy vegetables, cut them on the diagonal—this exposes them to more heat in the wok and they will cook more rapidly.

2. Choosing the right oil

Most oils with a high heating point can be used, such as sunflower, peanut, and vegetable oil, but avoid toasted sesame oil, as it has a low heating point and burns quickly—use it for seasoning your dishes. Olive oil isn't ideal because its flavor does not suit all Chinese dishes. It is best to use flavorless oil. My favorite is peanut—it has a slight nutty aroma that is not strong enough to overpower a dish, but acts as a great base on which to build layers of flavor.

3. The correct heat

To prepare the wok for stir-frying, heat it to high heat until it starts to smoke, then add the oil and swirl it around in the wok. During the cooking process, keep an eye on the flame and level of heat in the wok both before and after adding the food—the temperature in the wok will fall once the ingredients have been added, so you want the heat high enough to sear the food, but not so high that you burn the ingredients.

4. Adding raw ingredients and timing

The ingredients should go into the wok in the following order. Add the Chinese essentials such as garlic, ginger, and chilies first. Second, add the meat or seafood, and then, last, the vegetables, with a sprinkling of water to create steam. This order of cooking helps to retain the bite of the vegetables. It is important to dry the ingredients before you add them to the wok or the oil will spit, and if there is too much moisture, the ingredients will stew rather than fry. If you are using sauces or meats marinated in sauces, don't add the sauce or marinade until the end of the stir-frying process to ensure it doesn't all evaporate, and to prevent the food from stewing.

Sometimes the meat/protein is cooked first and then removed from the wok while the vegetables are stir-fried. It is then returned to the wok for the final mixing with seasoning. I find that you don't always have to cook in this way (recipes vary). There are some dishes where you can add the meat/protein after the garlic, ginger, and chilies and then, once they start to cook, you can add the rest of the ingredients; this helps to ensure that the meat/protein is not overcooked. So timing is important in wok cooking—knowing when the ingredient is ready for seasoning and when to add other ingredients. Work with what is best for you.

5. Adding cooked ingredients

Cooked noodles or cooked rice can be added to the wok at the end of the cooking process and combined with the rest of the ingredients, together with all the seasoning.

Steaming

Food cooked in a bamboo steamer takes on a subtle bamboo fragrance. This technique is a wonderful way of preparing a healthy meal; it's fast and fun too. You can also serve your food in the steamer, with the lid on; this helps to keep the food warm for longer.

1. Making sure the wok is stable

If you have a gas stove, invest in a wok rest; it helps to keep the wok stable and secure.

2. Filling the wok with water

Fill the wok (or a saucepan) half full with water and place the bamboo steamer over the top, making sure that the water doesn't touch the base of the steamer. Depending on the recipe, either place the food to be steamed directly in the steamer or on a heatproof plate. Put the lid on and steam. If necessary, add more boiling water as the food cooks.

3. Size of the bamboo steamer

Bamboo steamers vary in size, so make sure you buy one that sits snugly across the wok and will not touch the water. If necessary, you can sit the steamer on a heatproof plate, bowl, or rack in the wok to raise it above the water. For those who love to cook a feast, you can pile the steamers up as high as you want (although you will need a powerful flame that can produce enough steam to reach the highest steamer; I would say two or three piled high should be okay).

4. A final tip

Before you attempt to remove the lid of the steamer, make sure you always turn the flame off. I have been impatient many times and have burned my hands and arms from the hot steam.

Note: If you don't have a large enough bamboo steamer for the ingredient you want to cook (such as a large fish), place the food on a heatproof plate and put on a rack in a roasting pan. Carefully pour boiling water into the pan, then cover with foil and place in the oven. Cook for the time stated in the recipe at 400°F.

Deep-frying

You might think this not a very healthy way of cooking, but if the oil is hot enough, once the food is dropped in it will cook at such a high temperature that the outside edges are almost "sealed," not allowing the ingredient to absorb any more oil, and the high heat continues to cook the inside of the food. Some nonstick woks are not suitable for deep-frying; please check with the wok manufacturer. It's better to use a carbon steel wok that you can season yourself.

1. Making sure the wok is stable

If you are cooking on a gas stove, invest in a wok rest; this helps to keep the wok stable and secure—very important when deep-frying.

2. Making sure the oil is hot enough

To get the best results, use a deep-frying thermometer and follow the temperature stated in the recipe. If the oil isn't hot enough, the food will take longer to cook and be too oily. If the temperature is too hot, the food will burn and be undercooked on the inside. If you don't have a thermometer, then you can use the "bread test," which I refer to in my recipes. Be particularly careful when deep-frying in a wok—don't overfill it or leave it unattended.

3. Adding and removing the food

When lowering food into deep oil, I use a utensil called a spider. It is a web-like, woven steel mesh scooper that works well as a strainer. Use it also for lifting fried foods from the wok (draining much oil in the process) onto dishes lined with paper towels (again, to help drain excess oil). The spider comes in different sizes and you should be able to find it in all good Chinese supermarkets and kitchen/cookware shops. It often has a handle made of bamboo. Alternatively, you can use a slotted spoon or tongs, depending on the type of food being cooked.

4. Golden rules when deep-frying

- Make sure the food is dry, as this prevents spitting.
- For best results, never re-use oil.
- Use a large, long pair of bamboo chopsticks or metal tongs to help you turn food over if necessary (not plastic chopsticks, as they melt).
- Serve fried food immediately, as it will start to lose its crunch and crispness. However, if unavoidable, keep the food hot in a preheated oven before serving.

Other cooking utensils

The following would also be useful to have in the kitchen:

Wok cover

Invest in a wok cover; this will allow you to stew, steam, boil, and smoke food using your wok. It should have a handle on top and fit snugly and firmly on the wok.

Wok brush

This is a wooden brush with long hard bristles that is used with hot water to clean the wok. It's not essential but can take the hard work out of cleaning.

Chinese spatula/wooden spoon

Traditionally, a metal spatula is used to allow you to maneuver the food and scoop it out of the wok. This is fine for seasoned woks, but you may end up scratching off the nonstick coating if you use a nonstick wok. I would suggest a wooden spoon as an alternative.

Ladle

A Chinese ladle is small and bowl-shaped to allow you to scoop up soups and sauces from the wok, but I also use a normal ladle. Try to find one made from stainless steel, as carbon steel can rust easily.

Chinese cleaver/good knife

It is essential to invest in a good knife. I tend to use a medium-sized stainless-steel chef's knife made from one continuous piece of metal. However, I also have a stainless-steel Chinese cleaver with a wooden handle. Cleavers are particularly useful for hacking meat with bones and are also handy for slicing, shredding, dicing, mincing, and mashing (by using the side of the blade against the cutting board). Of course, you can use a food processor instead, but I find it is good therapy to chop away with the cleaver.

Cutting board

Choose a solid, large wooden cutting board and make sure you clean it well after use. I keep three different boards: one for meat, one for seafood, and one for fruits and vegetables.

Glossary

Unless otherwise stated, the ingredients should be available in most supermarkets.

Angelica sinensis (herb/dried)

Commonly known as Chinese angelica or dong quai, *Angelica sinensis* is grown in China and is widely used in traditional Chinese medicine to strengthen the blood and treat gynecological problems. All parts of the plant are used in cooking, including the leaves, stem, and roots. Dried pieces of the root are used in herbal soups, providing a strong woody aroma when cooked. Available from Chinese supermarkets.

Bamboo shoots (canned)

Drain canned bamboo shoots and use them in stir-fries and soups. They are rarely available fresh.

Basmati rice (dried)

Grown in India and Pakistan, basmati has a delicate, aromatic flavor. Being longer-grained than jasmine rice, it is less sticky when freshly cooked and so works well in fried-rice dishes. It is available as both white and brown rice. Both types can be used for a stir-fry, but for salads I prefer the brown variety, as it has more of a bite.

Black beans—*see* Fermented salted black beans

Black rice (dried)

Black rice—or "forbidden rice," as it is sometimes known, because in former times only the Chinese emperor was allowed to eat it—is particularly rich in iron and antioxidants (its color being a result of its high anthocyanin content). The rice is also ground to a fine powder to make black rice noodles. It has a deep nutty taste and is delicious in rice salads, adding texture and flavor as well as a striking contrast in color. Sometimes available from Western supermarkets, it can also be found in a good Chinese supermarket.

Black rice vinegar—*see* Chinkiang black rice vinegar

Bok choy (fresh)

This is a vegetable from southern China. The broad green leaves, which taper to white stalks, are crisp and crunchy. It can be boiled, steamed, or stir-fried in dishes.

Cassia bark—*see* Cinnamon stick/bark

Century eggs (preserved)

These are duck eggs (sometimes called thousand-year-old eggs) that have been buried in salt, tea leaves, and rice husk, covered with sodium bicarbonate, and left to age for 40–50 days. The yolk has a rich creamy texture and, when served chilled, the white is clear, jelly-like, and fragrant. Do not confuse these with preserved salted duck eggs—aged for 20 days, they have a deep orange yolk and an opaque, clean white.

Chili bean paste (sauce)

Mainly used in Sichuan cooking, this is made from soybeans and/or broad beans and chilies that have been fermented with salt to give a deep brown-red sauce. Some versions include fermented soybeans or garlic. This makes a great stewing sauce, but use with caution, as some varieties are extremely hot.

Chili oil (oil)

This is made from dried red chilies heated in oil to give a spicy orange-red fiery oil. Some chili oils also contain specks of dried chilies. Available from any Chinese supermarket, or you can make your own: heat a wok over medium heat and add some peanut oil. Add dried chili flakes with seeds and heat for 2 minutes. Take off the heat and leave to infuse in the oil until the oil has completely cooled. Decant into a glass jar with a tight lid and store for a month before using. For a clear oil, pass through a sieve.

Chili sauce (ingredient/dipping sauce)

This can be used in cooking or as a dipping sauce. There are several varieties; some are flavored with vinegar and garlic, such as Guilin chili sauce. For sweet chili sauce I use the Mae Ploy brand.

Chinese five spice/Chinese five-spice powder (spice)

This is a blend of cinnamon, cloves, Sichuan peppercorns, fennel, and star anise. These five spices give the sour, bitter, pungent, sweet, and salty flavors in Chinese cooking. The powdered form is great for marinades and when you want the flavors to be wholly incorporated into a dish. The whole spices can be crushed and used as a rub on meats as well as for flavoring oils.

Chinese wood ear mushrooms (dried)

These dark brown-black fungi have ear-shaped caps and are very crunchy in texture. They do not impart flavor, but add color and crispness to any dish. They should be soaked in hot water for 20 minutes before cooking—they will double in size. After soaking they should be rinsed well to remove any dirt. Store the dried pieces in a glass jar and seal tightly. Available from Chinese supermarkets.

Chinkiang black rice vinegar (condiment)

Made from fermented rice, this strong aromatic vinegar comes from Jiangsu province, where it is produced in the capital, Nanjing. The taste is mellow and earthy and gives dishes a wonderful smoky flavor. Balsamic vinegar makes a good substitute. Available from Chinese supermarkets.

Choy sum (fresh)

Closely related to bok choy, choy sum is a vegetable grown for its tender crunchy stalks and flavorful leaves, which are used in a whole range of dishes, especially soups and stir-fries. Available from Chinese supermarkets.

Cilantro (herb/fresh)

This is mainly used as a garnish or in soups, stir-fries, stews, and cold tossed salads. Both the leaves and stems of the herb are used.

Cilantro seeds (spice)

The dried seeds of the cilantro herb. When ground, they give a distinctive warm citrusy aroma to sweet and savory dishes.

Cinnamon stick/bark (spice)

This is the dried bark of various trees of the *Cinnamomum* genus, one of the more common being the cassia tree. It can be used in whole pieces or ground and is one of the components of Chinese five spice. "True" cinnamon, also known as Ceylon cinnamon, adds a sweet woody fragrance to any dish. Cassia bark is similar but has a woodier aroma; less expensive than cinnamon, it is more widely available and often sold in ground form as "cinnamon." Cinnamon is also said to have health-giving properties, such as preventing the common cold and aiding digestion.

Cloves (spice)

The clove tree is an evergreen and its dried flower buds are the aromatic spice that is one of the components of Chinese five spice. Cloves are strong and quite pungent in flavor. They are also used in traditional Chinese medicine to help digestion and promote the healthy function of the stomach, spleen, and kidneys.

Congee (dish)

A type of plain soupy rice or rice porridge. Can be combined with scrambled eggs, pickled turnip, salted peanuts, fermented bean curd (tofu ru), pickled cucumbers, and bamboo shoots pickled in chili oil.

Cumin (spice)

This is the dried seed of the herb *Cuminum cyminum*, and belongs to the parsley family. When ground the spice has a distinctive, slightly bitter but warm flavor.

Curry powder (spice)

There are many different blends of curry powder. Along with Chinese five-spice powder, some curry powders also include cilantro, turmeric, cumin, ginger, and garlic.

Daikon or white radish (fresh)

This grows in the ground like a root vegetable, and resembles a large white carrot. It has a peppery and crunchy taste and can be eaten raw, pickled, or cooked. Daikon contains vitamin C and diastase, an enzyme that helps digestion. It can be sliced or shredded and added to soups, salads, and stir-fries. The Koreans use this vegetable to make kimchi, their famous pickle. Store in a sealed bag—daikon has a pungent smell.

Dark soy sauce (condiment)

Made from wheat and fermented soybeans, dark soy sauce has been aged a lot longer than the light soy variety. It is mellower and less salty in taste than light soy, and is used to give flavor and color.

Deep-fried tofu (bean curd) (fresh)

This is fresh bean curd that has been deep-fried to a golden brown to make it crisp and crunchy on the outside. Usually found in the chilled sections of Chinese supermarkets.

Dried chili flakes (spice)

These are made from dried whole red chilies, including the seeds, which are crushed into flakes—they give a fiery heat when added to dishes.

Dried Chinese mushrooms (dried)

These have a strong aroma and need to be soaked in hot water for 20 minutes before cooking. They have a slightly salty taste and complement savory dishes well. After soaking, the stem can be left on or discarded. They are available from Chinese supermarkets. You can use dried shiitake or porcini mushrooms as a substitute.

Dried shrimp (dried)

These are shrimp that have been pre-cooked and then dried and salted to preserve them. To use, soak them in hot water for 20 minutes to soften them, then drain. Orange-red in color and very pungent in aroma and taste, they come in packets. As with all preserved ingredients, it is best to store them in an airtight container. Available from Chinese supermarkets.

Egg noodles (fresh/dried)
The most common type of noodle, they are made from egg yolk, wheat flour, and salt and come in various thicknesses and shapes. Some are flat and thin, others are long and rounded like spaghetti; some are flat and coiled in a ball. Available in various dried and fresh varieties. Store the fresh variety in the fridge for up to five days.

Enoki mushrooms (fresh)
These are tiny, white, very thin, long-stemmed mushrooms with a mild delicate flavor. When raw, they give great texture to salads. When lightly steamed, they are slightly chewy. They require very little cooking.

Fennel seeds (spice)
Fennel is a strong aromatic spice that has a slight aniseed aroma and flavor, but is much sweeter. It is one of the ingredients in Chinese five spice. Delicious when toasted or pan-fried and added to dishes.

Fermented bean curd (tofu ru) (preserved)
This is bean curd that has been preserved and flavored with chili, salt, and spices. It is often cubed, comes in many flavors, and white and red varieties are available. It is quite strong in flavor and is eaten on its own or used as a marinade, condiment, or an accompaniment to congee. Found in glass jars in Chinese supermarkets.

Fermented salted black beans (dried)
These are small black soybeans that have been preserved in salt and so they must be rinsed in cold water before use. A common ingredient, they are used to make black bean sauce and can be found in Chinese supermarkets. Only substitute black bean sauce if you can buy a very good-quality one; otherwise the dish won't taste the same.

Fish floss (dried)
Prepared in a similar way to pork floss, this is a form of dried shredded fish that is used as a topping for many savory dishes. Available from Chinese supermarkets.

Fish sauce (nam pla) (condiment)
Made from fermented fish, this is a staple ingredient in Southeast Asian cooking for curries, soups, and sauces.

Five spice/Five-spice powder—
see Chinese five spice/Chinese five-spice powder

Fresh bean curd (tofu) (fresh)
Described as the "cheese" of China, fresh bean curd is made from protein-rich bean curd. It is white and quite bland, but takes on the flavor of whatever ingredients it is cooked with. It is used as a meat substitute in a vegetarian diet. The texture is quite creamy and silky and there are various varieties, such as firm, soft, and silken. The firm variety is great in soups, salads, and stir-fries. Silken has a cream cheese–like texture. Tofu is protein-rich and contains B vitamins, isoflavones, and calcium. The fresh variety is usually found in the chilled sections of Chinese supermarkets and can be kept chilled in the fridge for up to one week.

Garam masala (spice)
This is a blend of ground spices (masala meaning "spice"), varying in its composition, but often including the spices that make up Chinese five spice. It is used widely in Indian cuisine and other South Asian dishes.

Glutinous rice (dried)
Grown throughout South Asia, this is a type of short-grain rice that is especially sticky (hence "glutinous" or "glue-like") when cooked. Available from Chinese supermarkets, it is used mainly in desserts.

Glutinous rice flour (ingredient)
Milled from glutinous rice, this is used in baking and as a thickener. Available from Chinese supermarkets.

Goji berries (dried)
Also known as wolfberries, these belong to the Solanaceae plant family (which includes potatoes, peppers, and tomatoes) and are native to southeastern Europe and Asia. Rich in antioxidants, they are used in traditional Chinese medicine to boost the immune system and improve blood circulation, among other applications. The dried berries, which have a sweet, licorice-like flavor, are added to herbal soups and congee, and brewed as a tea. (See also Matrimony vine.)

Hoisin sauce (sauce)
This is made from fermented soybeans, sugar, vinegar, star anise, sesame oil, and red rice (which gives it a slight red color). This is great used as a marinade and also as a dipping sauce.

Jasmine rice (dried)
This is a long-grain white rice that originates from Thailand. The rice has a nutty jasmine-scented aroma and makes a delicious accompaniment to dishes. As with most rice, you will need to rinse it before cooking until the water runs clear in order to get rid of any excess starch. White and silky, when cooked this rice is soft, white, and fluffy.

Kimchi (preserved)
This is a traditional side dish from Korea, written references to it going back 5,000 years. It consists of vegetables—such as cabbage, cucumber, or radishes—fermented or pickled with a variety of seasonings. Available from Chinese supermarkets.

Light soy sauce (condiment)
Light soy sauce is used in China instead of salt. It is made from fermented soybeans and wheat. A versatile and staple ingredient, it can be used in soups, stir-fries, and braised and stewed dishes. Wheat-free varieties, called tamari, are available for those with wheat intolerance, and there are also low-sodium varieties for those watching their sodium intake.

Ligusticum wallichii (herb/dried)
Commonly known as Sichuan lovage, the dried root of this plant is used in traditional Chinese medicine to improve blood circulation. It is often steeped in tea or added to herbal soups. Available from Chinese supermarkets.

Lily bulbs (dried)
Widely grown in China both for medicinal purposes and as a root vegetable, these are available mostly in dried form and therefore need to be pre-soaked in warm water for 20 minutes before cooking. Similar in texture to the potato but with a sweeter flavor, they are used in various dishes, including soups and stir-fries. Considered cooling or "yin" in character, the bulbs are regarded as especially suitable for eating in the summer. Available from Chinese supermarkets.

Lychee (fresh/canned)
Red or amber in color, oval in shape, and with a brittle skin, lychees are the fruit of an evergreen tree native to southern China. The translucent white or pinkish flesh is aromatic and has a distinctive flavor. In the center is a largish seed. Available fresh or canned.

Mantou (fresh/frozen)
A type of bun originating in northern China, where wheat rather than rice is grown as the staple food, *mantou* are made with wheat flour. Soft and fluffy in texture, they are steamed and used to accompany various dishes. They are available from the frozen section of Chinese supermarkets or can be bought fresh from Chinese bakeries.

Matrimony vine (herb/dried)
Also known as wolfberry (*see* Goji berries), the dried root is used in the same way medicinally as the dried fruit. It is used in herbal stews and soups with a variety of other herbs to boost the immune system. Available from Chinese supermarkets.

Miso paste (paste)
This is a thick paste made from fermenting rice, barley, soybeans, salt, and a fungus called *kojikin*. It comes in many varieties depending on the types of grains used to ferment the paste. It is used in Japanese soups and stocks and is sweet, earthy, fruity, and salty.

Momoya (paste)
Used mainly in Japanese cuisine, this is a paste made from edible seaweed mixed with soy sauce, sesame oil and seeds, mirin, red pepper, and garlic. Available from Chinese supermarkets, it makes a tasty garnish for rice dishes.

Mung bean noodles (dried)
Made from the starch of green mung beans and water, these noodles come in various thicknesses. Vermicelli is the thinnest type. Soak in hot water for 5–6 minutes before cooking. If using in soups or deep-frying, no pre-soaking is necessary. They become translucent when cooked. Great in salads, stir-fries, and soups, or even in spring rolls. Vermicelli rice noodles can be used as a substitute.

Oyster mushrooms (fresh)
These fungi are oyster-shaped, moist, hairless, and fragrant, and come in different colors—white, yellow, and gray. They are soft and chewy with a slight oyster taste—great in a stir-fry.

Oyster sauce (sauce)
This seasoning sauce made from oyster extract originated in the Canton province in China. It is used liberally on vegetable dishes and can be used as a marinade. A vegetarian variety, prepared from mushrooms, is also available. This is a very salty ingredient, so taste the dish before adding.

Panko breadcrumbs (ingredient)
Produced in Japan and made from bread without crusts, these have a crisper texture than other breadcrumbs. They are available from Asian stores and from many large supermarkets.

Peanut oil (oil)
This pale oil has a subtle, nutty flavor. It can be heated to high temperatures without burning and is great to use in a salad dressing. As an alternative, use vegetable oil.

Pickled bamboo shoots in chili oil (preserved)
These are bamboo shoots that have been pickled in vinegar, salt, and chili oil. They are great when used to flavor soups and stir-fries. They can usually be found in glass jars in Chinese supermarkets.

Pickled soy lettuce stems (preserved)
These are the stems of baby lettuce leaves that have been sliced and pickled in a soy brine. They have a

salty flavor and are delicious as an accompaniment for plain rice. They can also be chopped finely and used in stir-fries. Available from Chinese supermarkets.

Pork floss (dried)
Pork floss or *rousong* is a form of dried shredded meat used in China as a topping for a variety of dishes, including congee. Available from Chinese supermarkets.

Potato flour (ingredient)
Potatoes are steamed, dried, and then ground to give this silky-smooth white flour. It gives wonderful crispness to ingredients when they are coated in it before being pan- or deep-fried. It is gluten free. Sometimes called potato starch, it is available from Chinese supermarkets and some supermarkets. Cornstarch can be used as a substitute.

Preserved mustard greens/ Pickled Chinese cabbage (preserved)
The roots and leaves of the mustard cabbage are preserved with plenty of chili and salt. They are available in either jars, cans, or packets from Chinese supermarkets.

Preserved salted plums (preserved)
Much drier than prunes, these are eaten as a snack in China as well as used to make toppings and drinks. They are available from Chinese supermarkets in a variety of flavors.

Red dates (dried)
Also known as jujubes, these are the fruit of a small deciduous tree of the buckthorn family. When mature, the fruit are purplish-black and wrinkled-looking, like a small date. They are used in both traditional Chinese medicine (to alleviate stress) and Chinese cuisine—eaten as a snack or preserved and used in various dishes.

Rhizome of rehmannia (herb/ dried)
This is the dried root of a perennial herb, also known as the Chinese foxglove, used in traditional Chinese medicine to treat anemia, dizziness, and constipation. Sweetish in taste, the root is also added to herbal soups and tonic drinks. Available from Chinese supermarkets.

Rice vinegar (condiment)
Plain rice vinegar is a clear vinegar made from fermented rice. It is used in dressings and for pickling and is more common than black rice vinegar. Cider vinegar can be used as a substitute.

Sesame oil—*see* Toasted sesame oil

Sesame paste (paste)
This is made from crushed roasted white sesame seeds blended with toasted sesame oil to give a golden-brown paste, and is used with other sauces to help flavor dishes. If you cannot find this rich sesame paste, you can use tahini (the Middle Eastern equivalent) instead, but it is a lot lighter in flavor and so you will need to add more toasted sesame oil. Available from Chinese supermarkets.

Sesame seeds (ingredient)
These oil-rich seeds come from an annual plant, *Sesamum indicum*. They add a nutty taste and a delicate texture to many Asian dishes. Available in black, white/yellow, and red varieties, as well as toasted and untoasted—although they taste better freshly toasted.

Shaohsing rice wine (condiment)
This is wine made from rice, millet, and yeast that has been aged for between three and five years. Rice wine takes the "odor" or "rawness" out of meats and fish and gives a bittersweet finish. Dry sherry makes a good substitute.

Shi wheat-flour noodles (dried)
Shi means "thin/fine." The noodles are available in white and yellow varieties. The yellow variety has added coloring. They are great in soups, salads, and stir-fries. Use medium egg noodles as a substitute. Available from Chinese supermarkets.

Shiitake mushrooms (fresh)
These large dark-brown mushrooms are umbrella-shaped fungi that are prized for their culinary and medicinal properties. They contain all eight essential amino acids in more significant proportions than soybeans, milk, meat, and eggs, as well as vitamins A, B, B$_{12}$, C, and D, niacin, and minerals. They are a staple in China, Japan, and other parts of Asia, and are a popular source of protein.

Shimeji mushrooms (fresh)
Originating in East Asia, shimeji comprise a number of species. When cooked, they have a crunchy texture and nutty flavor that goes well in stir-fries, soups, and stews. Available from Chinese supermarkets.

Sichuan chilies/Dried chili flakes
There are many different varieties of Sichuan chilies—a common type is a short, fat, bright red chili that is hot and fragrant. They are usually sun-dried. You can grind the whole chilies using a mortar and pestle to make flakes.

Sichuan peppercorns (spice)
Known as *hua jiao* in Mandarin Chinese, or "flower pepper," these are the outer pod of a tiny fruit. They are widely used all over China and especially in western China. They can be wok-roasted, cooked in oil to flavor the oil, or mixed with salt as a condiment. They have a pungent citrusy aroma.

Sichuan preserved vegetables— see Preserved mustard greens/Pickled Chinese cabbage

Snake beans (fresh)
Snake beans or long beans are mostly grown in Asia. They are long, plump green beans, sometimes with a purple tinge to them, and since they are quite long, some varieties tend to twist. The fatter beans are more tender and sweet when cooked. This nutritious bean contains beta-carotene, vitamin C, and phosphorus, and the Chinese use this plant to make tonics for ailing kidneys or to treat stomach problems. They make a great accompaniment to many dishes.

Spring roll wrappers/pastry (fresh)
Made from wheat flour and starch, these are used for wrapping foods such as spring rolls before deep-frying. Available in the frozen sections of Chinese supermarkets. If you can find the type made with coconut oil and salt, they can be eaten raw, filled with salad and with dressings. Filo pastry makes a good substitute.

Star anise (spice)
A staple ingredient in Chinese cooking, these are called *bajiao* or "eight horns" in Chinese. They are the fruits of a small evergreen plant that grows in southwest China. Star anise has an aniseed flavor and is one of the ingredients found in Chinese five spice.

Toasted sesame oil (condiment)
Made from pressed and toasted white sesame seeds, this oil is used as a

flavoring and is not suitable for use as a cooking oil, since it burns easily. The flavor is intense, so use sparingly.

Tofu—see Fresh bean curd

Tofu ru—see Fermented bean curd

Turmeric (spice)
This is a tuberous rhizome of the ginger family. The rhizomes are first cooked for several hours and then dried before being ground into a powder, deep yellow in color. Turmeric imparts a strong yellow color to any dish and gives a slightly mustardy, peppery, earthy flavor. It also has medicinal properties and is used for its antiseptic properties for cuts and burns.

Udon noodles—see Wheat-flour flat udon noodles

Vermicelli mung bean noodles— see Mung bean noodles

Vermicelli rice noodles (dried)
Similar to vermicelli mung bean noodles, these come in many different widths and varieties. Soak in hot water for 5 minutes before cooking to soften. If using in salads, soak for 20 minutes. If using in a soup, add them dry. They turn opaque white when cooked. Great in soups, salads, and stir-fries.

Water chestnuts (canned)
Water chestnuts are the roots of an aquatic plant that grows in freshwater ponds, marshes, and lakes, and in slow-moving rivers and streams. Unpeeled, they resemble chestnuts in shape and coloring. They have a firm, crunchy texture. Sometimes available

vacuum-packed, they are mostly sold in cans.

Wheat-flour flat udon noodles (dried)
This is a thin, white wheat-flour noodle. Do not confuse these with the thick Japanese udon noodle. They are great in soups, salads, and stir-fries.

Wheat-flour pancakes (fresh)
Made from wheat flour, water, and salt and rolled into very thin discs, these are steamed before serving and accompany Peking duck and other dishes. They can be found in the frozen or chilled sections of any Chinese supermarket.

Wheat starch (dried)
Obtained from wheat grain, this white silken powder is combined with hot water and used to make dumpling skins that turn from opaque white to translucent white once steamed.

Wonton wrappers (fresh/ frozen)
Made from egg, wheat flour, salt, and water, these wrappers are used to make dumplings. They can be bought fresh or frozen from any Chinese supermarket.

Wood ear mushrooms—see Chinese wood ear mushrooms

Yellow bean sauce (sauce)
This is made from fermented yellow soybeans, dark brown sugar, and rice wine. It makes a great marinade for meats and a flavoring in many savory dishes.

Index

appetizers 38–73
asparagus and egg fried rice 186
avocado, fried eggs, and soy sauce, toast with 18, *19*

bacon lardons, shiitake mushrooms and chestnuts, red-cooked 112, *113*
bamboo shoots 229
   in chili oil, pickled 232
banana toffee fritters *214, 215*
basil:
   omelette with spicy sweet chili sauce 20
   plums and heirloom tomatoes with sweet basil and salted plum shavings 63
basmati rice 229
bean curd 46, *47*, 152, *153*, 230, 231, 234 *see also* tofu
bean paste, chili 229
bean sprout:
   black bean wok-fried ribs with chilies and 110, *111*
beef:
   with bean sprouts and scallions 102, *103*
   black pepper and rainbow vegetable stir-fry 104, *105*
   chili bean braised with cilantro and steamed mantou 162, *163*
   chili peanut 101
   curry in a hurry, Xi'an-style *106*, 107
   in oyster sauce with choy sum 100
   pancakes, crispy sweet chili *56*, 57
beef, pork, and lamb 96–117
berries, goji 231
big bowl of oat congee and accompaniments–"The Works" *24*, 25
black bean 229
   and chicken stir-fry 79
   fermented salted 231
   flounder steamed with *138*, 139
   mussels 122
   oriental mushrooms with 150
   wok-fried ribs with bean sprouts and chilies 110, *111*
black pepper beef and rainbow vegetable stir-fry 104, *105*
black rice vinegar 229, 230

boiled jasmine rice 184
bok choy 229
   with carrot and garlic 144
   shrimp and yellow bean chow mein with 202, *203*
   XO sauce and bok choy squid 130, *131*
   yellow bean and shrimp chow mein with 202, *203*
breadcrumbs, panko 232
breaded mackerel with Sichuan pepper, chili, and salt 134
breakfast 15–25
Buddha's stir-fried mixed vegetables 156
buns, roast pork brioche buns with caramelized red onions 172, *173*
buying and caring for your wok 223

Cantonese-style:
   roast duck and cucumber slices with salt and pepper 68, *69*
   roast duck with mango salad and plum dressing *70*, 71
   steamed lobster with ginger soy sauce 176, *177*
   sweet-and-sour pork 108
cassia bark 229
celery and tofu gan salad with sesame dressing 61
century eggs 229
char siu roast pork noodle soup 198, *199*
chestnuts, water 234
chicken:
   and black bean stir-fry 79
   and cashew nuts, chili 93
   with Chinese mushrooms, goji berries, and dried lily bulbs, steamed 85
   chow mein 197
   and duck 74–95
   General Tso's 80, *81*
   hoisin *88*, 89
   Kung Po 82, *83*
   oyster-sauce with ginger and shiitake mushrooms 86, *87*
   Sichuan chili tomato 84
   skewers, fried sweet chili 60
   three-cup 92
   twice-cooked salt and pepper 90, *91*
   yellow bean with green beans and shiitake mushrooms 78
chili:
   bean braised beef with cilantro and steamed mantou 162, *163*
   bean paste 229
   chicken and cashew nuts 93

crayfish tails and mango lettuce wraps 66, *67*
   dried Sichuan 233
   flakes, dried 230
   fried sweet chili chicken skewers 60
   oil 229
   peanut beef 101
   sauce 20, 229
Chinese cleaver/good knife 227
Chinese five spice 50, *51*, 229
Chinese fruity roast duck and wild rice salad 190
Chinese spatula/wooden spoon 227
Chinese sweet pork sausages with garlic 167
Chinese wood ear mushrooms 230
Chinese-style soft-shell crabs 54
Ching's life-changing Taiwanese liang mein 186
Ching's Yangzhou fried rice 188, *189*
Ching's zha jiang noodles 201
Chinkiang black rice vinegar 230
chow mein:
   with bok choy, shrimp, and yellow bean 202, *203*
   chicken 197
choy sum 230
   beef in oyster sauce with 100
   with oyster sauce, light 151
cilantro 230
   beef, chili bean braised with steamed mantou and 162, *163*
   hot sauce 50, *51*
   and pickled onion salad, spiced 175
   pickled whole radishes with 64
   pork rib, turnip, and carrot broth with 34, *35*
   salad 175
cinnamon stick/bark 230
clams:
   and Chinese sausage with bean sprouts and scallions 178, *179*
   mushroom and ginger wined 132, *133*
classic plain congee 191
cleaver, Chinese 227
cloves 230
cold sesame shrimp and cucumber 65
congee 230
   classic plain 191
   pork, ginger, and duck egg 23
country sausage, green pepper, and tomato fried rice with pineapple 22
crab:
   Chinese-style soft-shell 54
   and crayfish tail corn soup, posh 36
crackling pork shoulder with Chinese spices 164, *165*

crayfish:
    sweet chili noodles 204, *205*
    tail and crab corn soup, posh 36
    tails and mango lettuce wraps, chili 66, *67*
crispy seaweed 44
crispy sweet chili beef pancakes *56, 57*
cumin 230
curry:
    powder 230
    Xi'an-style beef in a hurry *106, 107*
cutting board 227

daikon or white radish 230
dark soy sauce 230
dates (dried), red 233
deep-fried tofu (bean curd) 230
deep-frying 226
dessert 206–21
dou miao with enoki mushrooms 148, *149*
dried chili flakes 230
dried Chinese mushrooms 230
dried shrimp 230–31
duck:
    Cantonese-style roast and cucumber slices with salt and pepper 68, *69*
    Cantonese-style roast with mango salad and plum dressing 70, *71*
    Chinese fruity roast and wild rice salad 190
    fruity sweet-and-sour 94, *95*
    mock and tender stem broccoli stir-fry 157

egg:
    century 229
    fried rice, asparagus, and 186
    fried rice, smoked salmon, and 21
    noodles 231
eggplant:
    fish-fragrant with pork *114*, 115
    fish-fragrant with tofu 152, *153*
enoki mushrooms 231
    dou miao with 148, *149*
equipment 221–7, *221, 228*

fennel seeds 231
fermented bean curd 231
fermented salted black beans 231
fish:
    floss 231
    -fragrant eggplant with pork *114*, 115
    -fragrant eggplant with tofu 152, *153*
    sauce (nam pla) (condiment) 231
fish & shellfish 118–19

five spice:
    Chinese 229, 231
    salted shrimp with hot cilantro sauce 50, *51*
floss, fish 231
flounder with black beans, steamed *138*, 139
flour:
    glutinous rice 231
    potato 233
fragrant star anise rice 184
fried rice:
    Ching's Yangzhou 188, *189*
    egg 21, 186
    green pepper and tomato 22
fried sweet chili chicken skewers 60
fritters, banana toffee *214, 215*
fruity sweet-and-sour duck 94, *95*
frying, deep 226

garam masala 231
General Tso's chicken 80, *81*
ginger and mushroom wined clams 132, *133*
glossary 229–34
glutinous rice 231
goji berries 231
green beans, sesame 62
green beans, yellow bean chicken with shiitake mushrooms and 78

Hakka-style pork belly 168, *169*
halibut with lemon sauce, Japanese-style crispy 52, *53*
hamburgers ("tiger bites pig"), Chinese with pickled cucumber *170, 171*
healthy sweet-and-sour jumbo shrimp stir-fry 126
heirloom tomatoes with sweet basil and salted plum shavings, plums and 63
hoisin:
    chicken *88*, 89
    sauce *88, 89*, 231

ice cream with exotic fruit, mango 217

Japanese-style crispy halibut with lemon sauce 52, *53*
jasmine rice 231
jumbo shrimp in chili tomato sauce with zucchini 127

kimchi 232
Kung Po chicken 82, *83*
knife 227

ladle 227
lamb:
    chops with pickled onion and cilantro salad, spiced *174, 175*
    stew, spicy 116, *117*
liang mein, Ching's life-changing Taiwanese 186
light choy sum with oyster sauce 151
Ligusticum wallichii (herb/dried) 232
lily bulbs 232
lobster, Cantonese-style steamed with ginger soy sauce 176, *177*
lotus root salad 145
lychee 232

mackerel, breaded with Sichuan pepper, chili, and salt 134
mango:
    and coconut pudding with orange cinnamon syrup 210, *211*
    ice cream with exotic fruit 217
    salad and plum dressing, Cantonese-style roast duck with 70, *71*
mantou 232
    beef, chili bean braised with cilantro and steamed 162, *163*
matrimony vine 232
miso paste 232
mock duck and tender stem broccoli stir-fry 157
momoya 232
mu shu pork 72, *73*
Mum's herbal eel soup 37
mung bean noodles (dried) 232
    vermicelli 234
mushroom:
    with black bean sauce, oriental 150
    Chinese wood ear 230
    dried Chinese 230
    enoki 231
    and ginger wined clams 132, *133*
    oyster 232
    shiitake 233
    shimeji 233
    wood ear 234
mussels, black bean 122

Nian gao 220–1, *221*
noodles 192–205
    Ching's zha jiang 201
    crayfish sweet chili 204, *205*
    egg 231
    mung bean 232
    shi wheat-flour 233
    Singapore 200
    udon 234

vermicelli mung bean 234
wheat-flour flat udon 234
nutty shrimp, asparagus, and cashew stir-fry 123

oat congee and accompaniments— "The Works," big bowl of 24, 25
oil:
  chili 229, 232
  peanut 232
  sesame 233
  sesame toasted 234
omelette, basil with spicy sweet chili sauce 20
oriental mushrooms with black bean sauce 150
oyster:
  mushrooms 232
  sauce 86, 87, 100, 151, 232
  sauce chicken with ginger and shiitake mushrooms 86, 87

pancakes:
  crispy sweet chili beef 56, 57
  wheat-flour 234
panko breadcrumbs 232
paste, sesame 233
peanut oil 232
peppercorns, Sichuan 233
pickled bamboo shoots in chili oil 232
pickled salad 151
pickled soy lettuce stems (preserved) 232–3
pickled whole radishes with cilantro 64
pineapple and mango crunch trifle 216
plum:
  apple and lychee spring rolls in cinnamon sugar 212, 213
  and heirloom tomatoes with sweet basil and salted plum shavings 63
  preserved salted 233
pork:
  belly, Hakka-style 168, 169
  brioche buns with caramelized red onions, roast 172, 173
  Cantonese-style sweet-and-sour 108
  fish-fragrant eggplant with 114, 115
  floss 233
  ginger and duck egg congee 23
  mu shu 72, 73
  mushroom and ginger wontons, watercress soup with 32, 33
  noodle soup, char siu roast 198, 199
  and shrimp fried wontons 58, 59
  rib, turnip, and carrot broth with cilantro 34, 35

salad, yin and yang crispy 109
sausages, Chinese sweet with garlic 167
shoulder with Chinese spices, crackling 164, 165
tenderloin with kimchi and enoki mushrooms 166
posh crab and crayfish tail corn soup 36
potato flour 233
preserved mustard greens/pickled Chinese cabbage (preserved) 233
preserved salted plums 233
pudding with orange cinnamon syrup, mango and coconut 210, 211

radishes with cilantro, pickled whole 64
red dates (dried) 233
red-cooked bacon lardons, shiitake mushrooms, and chestnuts 112, 113
rehmannia (herb/dried), rhizome of 233
rhizome of rehmannia (herb/dried) 233
ribs:
  black bean wok-fried with bean sprouts and chilies 110, 111
  pork rib, turnip, and carrot broth with cilantro 34, 35
  sweet-and-sour Wuxi 55
rice 180–91
  basmati 229
  boiled jasmine 184
  flour, glutinous 231
  fragrant star anise 184
  glutinous 231
  jasmine 231
  vinegar 233
  wine, Shaohsing 233
roast pork brioche buns with caramelized red onions 172, 173

salad:
  celery and tofu gan with sesame dressing 61
  Chinese fruity roast duck and wild rice 190
  lotus root 145
  mango salad and plum dressing 70, 71
  pickled 151
  yin and yang crispy pork 109
  zesty fruit salad with star anise syrup 218, 219
salmon and egg fried rice, smoked 21
sauce:
  black bean 150
  chili 20, 127, 229

cilantro hot 50, 51
dark soy 230
fish 231
ginger soy 176, 177
hoisin 231
oyster 86, 87, 100, 151, 232
soy 18, 19, 176, 177, 230, 232
spinach 136
XO 130, 131
yellow bean 18, 19, 128, 129
sausage:
  Chinese sweet pork sausages with garlic 167
  clams and Chinese with bean sprouts and scallions 178, 179
  country, green pepper, and tomato fried rice with pineapple 22
sea bass
  with ginger and mushrooms, steamed 135
  in spinach sauce, steamed 136
seaweed, crispy 44
seeds, sesame 233
sesame:
  green beans 62
  oil 233, 234
  paste 233
  seeds 233
  shrimp and cucumber, cold 65
  shrimp toast 45
  spinach, yellow bean 147
Shaohsing rice wine 233
shellfish & fish 118–39
shi wheat-flour noodles (dried) 233
shiitake mushrooms 233
shimeji mushrooms 233
  bacon lardons, and chestnuts, red-cooked 112, 113
  yellow bean chicken with green beans and 78
shrimp:
  in chili tomato sauce with zucchini, jumbo 127
  five-spice salted with hot cilantro sauce 50, 51
  healthy sweet-and-sour jumbo stir-fry 126
  nutty, asparagus, and cashew stir-fry 123
  and pork fried wontons 58, 59
  spicy sweet jumbo 124, 125
  toast, sesame 45
  and yellow bean chow mein with bok choy 202, 203
  with yellow bean sauce and garlic spinach, steamed jumbo 128, 129

shrimp, dried 230–31
Sichuan:
  chili tomato chicken 84
  chilies/dried chili flakes 233
  peppercorns 233
  preserved vegetables 234
  salt and pepper squid 48, 49
Singapore noodles 200
smoked salmon and egg fried rice 21
snake beans 234
soup:
  char siu roast pork noodle 198, 199
  Mum's herbal eel 37
  posh crab and crayfish tail corn 36
  tomato and egg flower 30
  traditional hot and sour 31
  watercress with pork, mushroom,
    and ginger wontons 32, 33
soups 26–37
soy lettuce stems, pickled 232–3
soy sauce:
  dark 230
  light 232
special mixed vegetables 154, 155
specials 158–79
spiced lamb chops with pickled onion
  and cilantro salad 174, 175
spicy lamb stew 116, 117
spicy sweet jumbo shrimp 124, 125
spinach, yellow bean sesame 147
spoon, Chinese spatula/wooden 227
spring roll:
  (chun juen), vegetable 42–3
  in cinnamon sugar, plum, apple, and
    lychee 212, 213
  wrappers/pastry 234
squid, Sichuan salt and pepper 48,
  49
star anise 234
  rice, fragrant 184
  zesty fruit salad with star anise syrup
    218, 219
starch, wheat 234
steamed chicken with Chinese
  mushroom, goji berries, and dried lily
  bulbs 85
steamed flounder with black beans
  138, 139
steamed jumbo shrimp
  with yellow bean sauce and garlic
    spinach 128, 129
steamed sea bass:
  with ginger and mushrooms 135
  in spinach sauce 136
steaming 228

stews, spicy lamb 116, 117
"stinky"-style aromatic tofu with
  kimchi 46, 47
stir-fry: 223–5
  bean sprout and scallion 144
  black bean and chicken 79
  black pepper beef and rainbow
    vegetable 104, 105
  healthy sweet-and-sour jumbo
    shrimp 126
  mixed vegetables, Buddha's 156
  nutty shrimp, asparagus, and
    cashew 123
  tender stem broccoli and mock duck
    157
sweet roasted vegetables 146
sweet-and-sour:
  duck, fruity 94, 95
  Wuxi ribs 55

Taiwanese liang mein, Ching's life-
  changing 186
techniques for cooking in a wok
  223–6
three-cup chicken 92
"tiger bites pig" (Chinese hamburgers)
  with pickled cucumber 170, 171
toast with avocado, fried eggs, and soy
  sauce 18, 19
toasted sesame oil 234
toffee banana fritters 214, 215
tofu (bean curd) 234
  deep-fried 230
  fish-fragrant eggplant with 152,
    153
  with kimchi, "stinky"-style aromatic
    46, 47
  ru 234
tomato:
  chicken, Sichuan chili tomato 84
  country sausage, green
    pepper, and tomato fried rice
    with pineapple 22
  and egg flower soup 30
  jumbo shrimp in chili tomato sauce
    with zucchini 127
  plums and heirloom tomatoes
    with sweet basil and salted plum
    shavings 63
traditional hot and sour soup 31
trifle, pineapple and mango crunch
  216
turmeric 234
twice-cooked salt and pepper chicken
  90, 91

udon noodles 234

vegetable:
  Buddha's stir-fried mixed 156
  Sichuan preserved 234
  special mixed 154, 155
  spring rolls (chun juen) 42–3
  stir-fry, black pepper beef and
    rainbow 104, 105
  sweet roasted 146
vegetarian 142–57
vermicelli mung bean noodles
  234
vinegar:
  black rice 229
  Chinkiang black rice 230
  rice 233

water chestnuts 234
watercress soup with pork, mushroom,
  and ginger wontons 32, 33
wheat starch 234
wheat-flour:
  flat udon noodles 234
  pancakes 234
white radish 230
wine, Shaohsing rice 233
wok 221
  buying and caring for your 223
  cover 227
wonton:
  pork, mushroom, and ginger,
    watercress soup with 32, 33
  shrimp and pork fried 58, 59
  wrappers 234
wood ear mushrooms 234
"The Works" 24, 25
Wuxi ribs, sweet-and-sour 55

Xi'an-style beef curry in a hurry 106,
  107
XO sauce and bok choy squid 130,
  131

yellow bean:
  chicken with green beans and
    shiitake mushrooms 78
  and shrimp chow mein with bok choy
    202, 203
  sauce 234
  sesame spinach 147
yin and yang crispy pork salad 109

zesty fruit salad with star anise syrup
  218, 219

Acknowledgments

I owe a huge thank you to all the cooks who have supported me throughout my career. It warms my heart whenever I receive a friendly, kind message of love and support and it gives me great confidence and joy; I dedicate this book to you all. I hope this book will come in handy in the kitchen and give you more happy days of wokking to come. I also share some more of my stories with you.

From my very first beginnings on Great Food Live on the Good Food Channel, I owe another big thank you to Fiona Cho, who helped me as a true friend, believed in what I could achieve, and allowed me to realize my dream and potential. I would not be where I am without your burst of inspiration and enthusiasm all those years ago. I am forever grateful.

Thank you to Toby Eady and everyone at Toby Eady Associates—Jamie Coleman, Zaria Rich, and Nicole—for your unconditional love and support, and for continuing to champion me! To Michael Foster, Alexandra Henderson, and Katie Rice at PFD, who have helped me so much in the last year through some difficult times, thank you for all your hard work and belief.

This book would not have been possible without the special help and support of so many people. I would like to thank you from my heart for giving me this amazing opportunity to continue to do what I love— Victoria Barnsley, Belinda Budge, my (incredibly smart and beautiful) publisher Carole Tonkinson, my project editor Georgina Atsiaris and copyeditor Kate Parker, cover designer Richard Augustus, and layout designer Sophie Martin. Thank you also to Liate Stehlik, Cassie Jones, and everyone at HarperCollins US for making my dream come true.

Thanks to Jennifer Joel and Michael Kagan at ICM Talent in the US for helping to open up opportunities for me and for believing in me. Thank you for your incredible patience. Thanks to Tybalt Whitney—I have learned a lot from you!

To all my family, Buddhist masters, friends, fans, cooks, and chefs who have helped me on my journey, past and present, I am indebted and ever grateful—special mentions to Sir David Tang KBE; Alan Yao OBE; Wing Yip OBE; David Mulcahy, Vice President of Craft Guild of Chefs; Holland and Andy Kwok of Good Earth Restaurant; and Jayne Hibbit.

Thanks to all the powers at Good Food Channel, BBC, Channel 5, and Cooking Channel (Bruce Seidel, Michael Smith), and the producers at Lion TV (Richard Shaw), Blink TV (Dan Chambers), and Optomen TV for continuing to give me opportunities and allowing me to share my cooking!

To Jamie—I can't believe we did this book together! This book will always be special to me because we both slaved over it—a labor of love, with me cooking every dish and you capturing it. However imperfect, it is perfect; thank you from my heart.

To Choi sum and Paco, I love your cankering and ankle-nipping antics when I'm washing up; thank you for your unconditional cuteness and love!